IMAGES OF WA

CW00797442

ARMOURED WARFARE
IN THE
FIRST WORLD WAR
1916–1918

British troops gather around their supporting tank – it was designed to cross trenches and break the deadlock on the Western Front.

IMAGES OF WAR

ARMOURED WARFARE
IN THE
FIRST WORLD WAR
1916–1918

RARE PHOTOGRAPHS FROM
WARTIME ARCHIVES

Anthony Tucker-Jones

Pen & Sword
MILITARY

First published in Great Britain in 2016 by
PEN & SWORD MILITARY
an imprint of
Pen & Sword Books Ltd,
47 Church Street,
Barnsley,
South Yorkshire
S70 2AS

Text copyright © Anthony Tucker-Jones, 2016
Photographs copyright © as credited, 2016

Every effort has been made to trace the copyright of all the photographs.
If there are unintentional omissions, please contact the publisher in writing, who
will correct all subsequent editions.

A CIP record for this book is available from the British Library.

ISBN 978 147387 298 1

The right of Anthony Tucker-Jones to be identified as Author of this Work has
been asserted by him in accordance with the Copyright, Designs and Patents Act
1988.

All rights reserved. No part of this book may be reproduced or transmitted in any
form or by any means, electronic or mechanical including photocopying, recording
or by any information storage and retrieval system, without permission from the
Publisher in writing.

Typeset by CHIC GRAPHICS

Printed and bound by CPI Group (UK) Ltd, Croydon, CR0 4YY

Pen & Sword Books Ltd incorporates the imprints of Pen & Sword Archaeology,
Atlas, Aviation, Battleground, Discovery, Family History, History, Maritime, Military,
Naval, Politics, Railways, Select, Social History, Transport, True Crime, Claymore
Press, Frontline Books, Leo Cooper, Praetorian Press, Remember When, Seaforth
Publishing and Wharncliffe.

For a complete list of Pen & Sword titles please contact
Pen & Sword Books Limited
47 Church Street, Barnsley, South Yorkshire, S70 2AS, England
E-mail: enquiries@pen-and-sword.co.uk
Website: www.pen-and-sword.co.uk

Contents

Introduction: Germany's Downfall

The story of the creation of the tank is one of pioneering innovation, frustrated military aspirations and lost opportunities. At the time, rather surprisingly, it did not lead to an arms race because the other side chose to ignore it. What follows is designed to provide both a visual guide and brief assessment of the birth of modern armoured warfare. Despite contributing to the defeat of Imperial Germany in 1918, the latter ironically sowed the seeds for the Nazi concept of Blitzkrieg. Although the Battle of Cambrai is held up as the very first tank battle this is in fact a myth, as tanks had already fought at Flers-Courcelette during the Somme offensive, Arras, Passchendaele and Berry-au-Bac. Nor was it the largest tank battle, as the Allied sledgehammer assault at Amiens involved far greater numbers.

The tank concept was developed as a solution to the dreadful impasse that developed on the Western Front during the First World War. British innovation was driven by the need to overcome enemy trenches and strongpoints: indeed by the time the Germans developed their own tanks the first tank-to-tank actions were but a footnote to the conflict.

Although the origins of modern armoured and mechanized warfare date from the First World War, it was not an easy birth. Britain, France and Germany developed armoured fighting vehicles that universally became known as the tank to help break the deadlock of trench warfare. The British and French easily led the way as the Germans were well behind the curve. Getting the balance of power-to-weight ratio and armament just right proved to be a very tricky and often deadly business. Apart from the British Whippet and the French FT all the tanks of this period were little more than lumbering landlocked battleships. Nonetheless, their use at Cambrai and Amiens showed the way ahead.

Essentially First World War British heavy tanks were designed as a breakthrough weapon akin to the later heavy German Tiger and Soviet KV tanks of the Second World War. It was the French who subsequently ran with the concept of a light tank during the First World War intended to exploit a breakthrough. Both British heavy and French light tanks achieved mixed results during 1916–18 but they laid the foundations for all future armoured and mechanized warfare.

Throughout history cavalry had played an often decisive part in battle by combining mobility, protection and offensive power. They regularly brought terror to the enemy by turning a flank, exploiting a breakthrough and by pursuing a demoralized and defeated army. Led by noblemen and gentlemen, the thrill was in the chase. Eventually improvements in firearms technology inevitably meant that the weight of the fighting always rested on the infantry. In the aftermath of the Napoleonic Wars the introduction of the rifle gave the infantry a weapon with a range of 1,000 yards that spelt the end of the cavalry charge. Likewise the evolution of artillery and artillery tactics changed how cavalry were used.

By the time of the American Civil War cavalry were increasingly being employed as mounted infantry or dragoons. Europe learned the hard way during the Franco-Prussian War that the cavalry charge was now all but redundant in the face of devastating firepower. Similarly the British Army also learned the same lesson in South Africa during the Boer War. Mounted Boer riflemen easily outfought British cavalry who persisted in keeping the lance and sabre. It was only when the British deployed large numbers of mounted units which fought dismounted that the Boers were finally defeated. At the beginning of the First World War such lessons were largely ignored across much of Europe.

On the eve of war Europe was still hopelessly in love with the glamour and dash of the cavalry. It was a career that appealed to many of Europe's aristocracy. On the Western Front some ten French and one British cavalry divisions found themselves confronted by a similar number of German cavalry divisions. Initially, as a result of the Schlieffen Plan, the war was very fluid with the German armies swinging rapidly through Belgium. Very briefly the cavalry and horse artillery had their moment of glory.

Once the German advance had been stopped on the Aisne, the fighting took on a completely different complexion. The cavalry became separated and hemmed in by vast trench systems that they were powerless to prevent being constructed. Again the generals failed to appreciate that the need was for mobile mounted riflemen, not old-style European cavalry still brandishing the lance and sabre as if it were yesteryear.

Cavalry became useless and infantry assaults supported by massive artillery bombardments the order of the day. The battlefield was churned up and shorn of all vegetation turning it into a desolate lunar like landscape. Once the rains came the area between the opposing trenches turned into a sea of mud and became called No Man's Land for good reason. Both the British and French generals decided that attack was the best form of defence and proceeded to fight a war of attrition against the German defences. Their aim was to wear Germany down no matter the appalling cost in human lives.

In 1915 both sides tried to break the deadlock by resorting to poison gas. The Germans first used it at the Second Battle of Ypres when they gassed the British in the Ypres Salient. The British then employed it during the Battle of Loos. It proved not to be a decisive weapon and simply added to the suffering and misery of those in the trenches. Both sides quickly learned how to cope with this new horror. By 1916 there was deadlock and in desperation the British and the French began secretly developing the 'tank' in an effort to break through on the Somme.

The popular perception is that Winston Churchill was the founding father of the tank, an accolade which he thoroughly enjoyed. In fact Ernest Swinton and David Lloyd George were the greatest driving forces, Swinton for his tenacity in pushing the concept forward and Lloyd George for ensuring the Army did not thwart the programme at the crucial moment after the second phase of the Battle of the Somme. Hugh Elles, John Fuller and John Monash also featured prominently as pioneers in the evolution of the world's very first tank force – the British Tank Corps. In France Jean Estienne was the leading light in creating French tanks. Likewise George Patton Jr was responsible for forming America's very first tank units.

Field Marshal Sir Douglas Haig remains a controversial figure thanks to his command of the British Expeditionary Force and his conduct of the war on the Western Front. His name will forever be associated with the slaughter on the Somme. However, it was he who advocated the expansion of the Tank Corps. In contrast Haig's superior, the Chief of the Imperial General Staff General Sir William Robertson, and his subordinate General Sir Henry Rawlinson were far from enthusiastic supporters of the tank concept. If anything Haig was over-optimistic about the fledgling tank's capabilities. On the other hand Rawlinson was initially completely baffled by it.

Following their success against the Russians Generals Hindenburg and Ludendorff were sent to command the Western Front. They moved to strengthen German defences and behind their front lines created new fortifications known as the Hindenburg Line. Once this was complete they withdrew to these much stronger defences in early 1917. This resulted in another dreadful slogging match with British tanks failing to deliver the desired result at the Battle of Cambrai.

The tank did not come of age until 1918. Morale in the German Army by this stage was poor and desertion rife. The German high command's reactionary thinking when it came to this newfangled armoured warfare served the common soldier poorly. Even though German generals scoffed at the utility of Britain and France's tanks, soldiers were calling them *Deutschland's Tod* or 'Germany's Downfall'.

While the Allies were producing tanks in ever-growing numbers the Germans were slow to follow and failed to develop really effective anti-tank tactics and weapons. Only after the French Army's use of masses of Renault tanks during the counter-attacks on the Marne did the German high command reverse its thinking. By this stage in the fighting it was simply too late. Instead Ludendorff pinned his hopes in victory on his 'stormtroopers' who spearheaded the German Spring Offensive of 1918. While the results were remarkable, they were not enough.

The Allies launched a surprise attack on 8 August 1918 at Amiens that heralded the end of the First World War. This was supported by over 600 tanks, the largest number to have ever been active in any of the battles of the conflict. In total the British Army committed a dozen tank battalions and they along with over twenty Allied divisions left 500,000 German casualties in their wake. Just 100 days later the war came to an end with the Armistice on 11 November 1918. The tank had proved to be Germany's downfall.

Photograph Sources

All photos in this book are sourced via the author.

Chapter One

'Little Willie' and 'Mother'

By the spring of 1915 the fighting on the Western Front had reached an impasse. The initial war of mobility and manoeuvre had stagnated into static warfare – artillery, machine guns and barbed wire became kings of the battlefield. Attempts by the British to break through at Ypres failed and it was decided that brute force and attrition was the way to defeat Germany. The German military concluded, after the use of poison gas had failed to achieve the desired results, that they would remain on the defensive while they concentrated on the Eastern Front and the war against Imperial Russia and her allies.

British boffins needed to find a solution to what had become effectively siege warfare on the Western Front. To break the deadlock they turned to the one device that had dominated the first half of the twentieth century – the internal combustion engine, which ironically had been created by the Germans Karl Benz and Gottlieb Daimler in 1885. Lorries and buses had already been pressed into service to ferry troops and supplies to the front. These vehicles, while a great help, struggled to cope with the mud near the front.

On the face of it the logical solution was to replace the cavalry's horses with armoured cars. Not that the cavalry regiments would have countenanced such heresy. These could have roared up and down the roads mowing down enemy cavalry and infantry. The snag was that armoured cars, like all automobiles of the day, were only suitable for on-road use. The creation of the trenches and No Man's Land soon put paid to any such notions.

Behind the lines the British Royal Navy deployed armoured cars to protect its naval air squadrons based at Dunkirk. Initially they were little more than motorcars strengthened by sheets of mild steel boiler plating. Companies such as Rolls-Royce, Wolseley and Lanchester produced custom-built armoured cars in late 1914 but these were designed to run on roads. While vehicles such as the Rolls-Royce armoured car were useful for security duties, they quickly proved a failure as mechanized cavalry because they could not cope with shell-blasted battlefields.

The Austin Motor Company also built an armoured car in 1914 with twin machine-gun turrets. This four-man vehicle had rear-axle drive and was based on a civilian car chassis. However, this was specifically designed for the Russian Army. The British only ever used just over a dozen Austins in 1918 after the Russian Revolution disrupted deliveries.

By chance, the official British war correspondent Lieutenant Colonel Ernest Swinton stumbled upon an American invention in October 1914 that was to change the face of warfare forever. He was informed about the 10-ton Holt caterpillar tractor by an acquaintance who had seen one in Antwerp. Swinton was in fact something of a trench warfare expert, having written the official British military history of the Russo-Japanese War. This conflict had resulted in the first trench stalemate of the twentieth century. In a quirk of history American inventor Benjamin Holt had first demonstrated his working tracked tractor in November 1904. His subsequent designs drew on the British Hornsby caterpillar artillery tractor, which the War Office had proved uninterested in. Lacking customers, Hornsby sold its patents to Holt.

Swinton foresaw how the Holt caterpillar could cope with the mud and reasoned that if such a vehicle was armoured and armed it could overcome German barbed wire and machine guns. He presented his ideas to British General Headquarters (GHQ) in France, which fell on deaf ears. Undeterred Swinton then sent a copy of his report to a close friend, Lieutenant Colonel Maurice Hankey in London, who was Secretary to the Committee of Imperial Defence. Hankey was impressed and sought to lobby the Royal Navy who at the time had responsibility for all issues regarding fighting motor vehicles.

In January 1915 Hankey's memorandum landed on the desk of one Winston Churchill, then First Lord of the Admiralty. Churchill liked the idea and went to the Prime Minister Herbert Asquith. Churchill reasoned that Lord Kitchener, Secretary of State for War, must embrace such ideas if the Army was ever to storm the enemy defences. Kitchener was persuaded to set up a small body of experts who were tasked with evaluating the Holt tractor's capabilities. The trials using a trailer did not go well and the War Office remained unconvinced, no doubt influenced by its experiences with the Hornsby tractor.

In response to lobbying by the Royal Navy Air Service (RNAS), which was operating the armoured cars in France, Churchill set up the Admiralty Landships Committee to explore their concepts further. This involved tracked and big-wheel vehicles. Lieutenant Albert Stern from the RNAS Armoured Car Division became the committee's secretary. As a result of the Admiralty's involvement naval terminology became the accepted norm when describing elements of what was to became the tank, such as bow, deck, hull, turret and superstructure.

Swinton, having returned to France, tried once more to interest GHQ in his ideas. He submitted a new paper entitled *The Armoured Machine Gun Destroyer* that seemed to strike a chord. This was sent to the War Office's Inventions Committee which had been set up to examine such new ideas. By the summer of 1915 Swinton was back in London as the Secretary to the Dardanelles Committee and it was at this point he learned of the existence of the Admiralty Landships Committee. By now a prototype vehicle had been built by Fosters of Lincoln, which produced heavy artillery tractors for the Royal Marines. This prototype based on the American Bullock Creeping Grip Caterpillar was to result in 'Little Willie'. Both suffered from problems with their tracks because they were inadequate for the vehicle's size.

As is often the case with new ideas, a turf war broke out. David Lloyd George's Ministry of Munitions felt that the Admiralty Committee was meddling beyond their remit. In order to head off the dissension, the Prime Minister instructed the two sides to pool their resources and the Joint Experiments Committee was established. The Landships Committee was eventually reorganized as the Tank Supply Committee under the chairmanship of Lieutenant Stern with Swinton as a member.

Lloyd George turned out to be an enthusiastic champion of the tank and did all he could to support its development and deployment. At the start of the First World War he was serving as the Chancellor of the Exchequer. In the Spring of 1915 Lloyd George had become the Minister of Munitions, the following summer he was appointed Secretary of State for War then became Prime Minister at the end of 1916.

A team headed by Fosters Chairman William Tritton and Lieutenant W. G. Wilson (from the RNAS Armoured Car Division) in September 1915 managed to resolve the troublesome issues with 'Little Willie's' tracks and produced 'Big Willie' or 'Mother'. To ensure secrecy the chassis and hull were built at different locations – with the hull being referred to as a water carrier or water tank for use in Mesopotamia. While everyone was scratching their heads to come up with a suitable name for this new armoured fighting vehicle, Swinton suggested simplicity itself and coined the term 'tank'. 'Mother' was to become the basis for the very first British production tank.

Key to the evolution of 'Big Willie' was its ability to get over enemy trenches and stay in the fight. Essentially it needed to be a breakthrough weapon as well as infantry support weapon. As the Germans at this stage of the war had not developed their own tanks it was not envisaged that the new British vehicle would have to cope with tank-to-tank combat. Being able to cross enemy trenches was its key role and this impacted on the shape and general appearance of what was to become the first British tank.

Churchill, after the debacle of the Dardanelles Expedition against Turkey, lost his job as First Sea Lord. He decided to return to soldiering and was deployed to the Western Front as second-in-command of a Guards battalion. This gave him first-hand experience of the problems facing the British and French armies. While in France Churchill continued to champion the tank concept. Later John Oborne, serving with the 4th Battalion, Devonshire Regiment, was grateful for Churchill's persistence, 'You had a certain amount of shielding because you used to follow the tanks along. They were a great help. They'd flatten the wire. I know they were in their infancy, but Churchill did a good job with them.'

When a final field demonstration of 'Mother' took place in England General Sir Douglas Haig, commanding British forces in France, sent an officer on his staff as his official observer. The veteran Major Hugh Elles had been commissioned into the Royal Engineers. While serving as a staff officer in France he had seen action at the Battle of the Aisne and had been wounded at the Second Battle of Ypres. Elles was impressed by 'Mother' and reported favourably back to Haig. The success of this trial prompted Lloyd George, who was then still Minister of Munitions, to put the tank into production.

Above and left:
By 1915 the fighting on the Western Front had reached a stalemate thanks to trench warfare dominated by mud, the machine gun, artillery and barbed wire. Something was needed to break it.

Belgium was one of the first countries to deploy the armoured car with its Minerva Model 1914 seen here outside Antwerp. However, armoured cars could not operate off-road so had limited utility on the Western Front.

Prior to the First World War, the British company Hornsby developed a caterpillar artillery tractor. The military were not interested so Hornsby sold its patents to the American Holt Company.

Holt tractors towing British artillery – without them there would have been no tank.

The Holt 75 model gasoline-powered caterpillar tractor provided the inspiration for the tank. It was used from 1915 by both the British and French armies as an artillery tractor. The front tiller wheel was discontinued on the later models.

David Lloyd George, as firstly Minister of Munitions and subsequently Secretary of State for War then Prime Minister, was an ardent supporter of the development of the tank.

An engineering friend told official British war correspondent Lieutenant Colonel Ernest Swinton in the summer of 1914 that he had seen the American Holt Caterpillar tractor in Antwerp. On 19 October 1914, whilst driving through France, Swinton came up with the idea of a tracked armoured fighting vehicle.

The Number 1 Lincoln Machine prototype built by William Foster & Company made its first test run on 9 September 1915. Problems with the tracks led to 'Little Willie'.

Built by Foster & Co Little Willie was Britain's second prototype tank. The wheels on the back were to help with steering. Development of this design led to the very first British Mark I tank.

Chapter Two

Male and Female

The very first British tank went into service in 1916, exactly two years after the outbreak of the First World War. Its rather peculiar and very distinctive rhomboid shape was to ensure a long track run capable of crossing the vast trench networks on the Western Front. The tracks ran around the outer edges of the entire hull and could manage a very modest 3.7mph. Speed was not really an issue as the tank was intended to match the pace of the infantry. The resulting height of the hull meant a turret would have made the vehicle top heavy, so the main armament was placed in sponsons on either side. It was dubbed rather unimaginatively the Mark I of which just 150 were built in two types.

The male, weighing in at 31 tons, was armed with two 6-pounder naval guns mounted in side sponsons and four Hotchkiss machine guns in ball mounts. The female weighed only slightly less at 30 tons and was armed with six machine guns. The idea was that the males could deal with enemy defences, fortifications and guns while the females went after enemy troops.

The Mark I male was easily distinguishable from other marks of British heavy tank because of the length of its gun barrels. The 6-pounders were the original Admiralty pattern 8cwt 40 calibre, but these were replaced in the Mark IV onwards with the shorter 6 cwt 23 calibre gun the barrel of which was less likely to get stuck in the mud or damaged by buildings and trees. It could traverse 100° from dead ahead and had a muzzle velocity of 554m/sec compared to 441m/sec for the 23-calibre gun. Ammunition carried consisted of High Explosive (HE), Armour Piercing (AP) and case shot (anti-personnel for use against infantry in the open) and totalled up to 332 rounds. The initial naval guns had a far greater range than was really necessary for the tank's role.

The Mark I (and subsequent marks) featured a raised cupola in the hull front for the driver and the commander, who also served as brakesman. External features peculiar to the Mark I included the protective bomb roof and wheeled steering tail. The former comprised a wood or metal frame covered in chicken wire mounted on the hull roof to deflect grenades. This subsequently proved unnecessary and was discarded. The steering tail was introduced on the prototypes to help with steering and stability. It comprised two iron-spoked wheels fitted to an Ackerman steering axle, which was controlled from a steering wheel in the driver's position by wires. The idea was the rudder action of the tail could accomplish minor course-corrections or large-radius turns without resorting to a gear-change on the tracks. This steering unit could be raised from the ground for transport.

The engine, a Daimler 105hp petrol type, was mounted in the centre of the hull. This was served by a two-speed gearbox with a differential drive to the two cross shafts at the front and back. These were joined to the four 'horns' of the tank, in particular to the rear drive sprockets by chain drive and reduction gear. A tubular water radiator was installed behind the engine with the fan driven by the engine. The exhausts were fitted to holes in the roof. In an effort to dissipate sparks and smoke twin baffle plates were installed.

The designers were rightly proud of themselves and there is no denying that the Mark I looked a formidable beast. It could cross enemy trenches up to 11ft wide and tackle obstacles up to 4ft tall. However, they were not given sufficient time to iron out the inevitable teething problems or indeed fine-tune the overall design. The necessities of war ensured that the very first British tank, like so many that were to follow it, was rushed into combat before it was really ready.

The weight of the tank placed a tremendous strain on the drive train, which resulted in it being mechanically unreliable. Notably, climbing up steep inclines caused fuel starvation due to the gravity fuel feed system. The fuel also presented the risk of fire especially as the petrol tanks were mounted high in the hull. The gun sponsons could be unbolted for transportation in order to reduce the weight and width, but as each weighed 1 ton 15cwt this was no easy task. Access was not easy either. There was a manhole opening in the roof, but normally the crew clambered in and out of the vehicle via the doors in the rear of the sponsons. The steering tail while useful on good ground could not cope with the realities of No Man's Land. Following the Mark I's debut on the Somme it was decided to discard the tails in November 1916, steering solely by gear-changes.

In addition, the fighting compartment for the eight-man crew was a hellish place to be. Many of the new crews had in fact not seen action on the Western Front, so were not sure what to expect and they were drawn from all branches of the army. For a start it was impossible for them to stand upright and after half an hour running the massive engine the temperature could reach well over 100°F. To counter this crews gulped down up to a gallon of water per man per day. Although fume outlet louvres were cut into the rear of the vehicle, fresh air for the engine had to be drawn in from the crew openings in the hull. Noxious fumes from the engine soon filled the interior and made the crews delirious and nauseous. As with all tankers down through the ages if they wanted to urinate during combat they had to resort to a spent shell case.

Not only was the ventilation poor, so was the visibility. The vision devices were crude, consisting of just slits or flaps. The ride was rough as the tracks were not sprung. The armour posed a danger to the crew as the plates were riveted to unarmoured girders and angle irons. This meant that when the joins were hit even by small-arms fire the crew with be subject to 'splash' or spalling by the rivets and armour.

Noise from the petrol engine was such that verbal communication was impossible. The driver had to relay his orders to the two gearsmen by hammering a set code on the engine cover. Gunner A. H. R. Reiffer, MM who fought in a Mark I at Flers recalled, 'There was hell outside all right, but there was such a hell of a noise inside and we were such a tight-packed crew, that we didn't concern ourselves with what was happening outside.'

The tank had to be steered either by putting one track into neutral and the other into first or second gear, or by applying the brake on one side. Both had their disadvantages. Using the gears caused the tank to lurch round violently, while using the brake was exhausting for the brakesman and rapidly wore out the brakes. Using the clutch method of steering required four crewmen, the driver, brakesman and the two gearsmen. Separate gear operators were required for each track. Once the tank had turned, to ensure straight running another gear switch was required. Doing all this while under fire and in boggy conditions made the whole procedure even more difficult.

Production was slow and it was not until July 1916 that the first tanks left the factories. The following month just fifty were shipped to France. Under great secrecy crews had to be recruited and trained to man the Mark I. To try and hide what was going on this new organization was initially called the Armoured Car Section, Motor Machine Gun Service, then renamed for greater secrecy the Heavy Section, Machine Gun Corps. In light of the tanks being equipped with machine guns this did not seem too unreasonable. The 'Heavies' comprised 184 officers and 1,600 men, and they and their tanks were divided into six companies of four sections, each section consisting of three male and three female tanks.

Initial crew training in Britain was conducted at the Bisley ranges in Surrey, but once they had their first tanks they moved to Thetford, Norfolk on the estate of Lord Iveagh. It was from here that the first three companies departed for France in the summer of 1916. Toward the end of the year Bovington Camp, at Wool in Dorset, was selected as the new home of Britain's very first tank force. The Mark I was blooded at the Battle of Flers-Courcelette, part of the renewed Somme offensive, on 15 September 1916.

British heavy tank designations ran from the Mark I through to the Mark X, though the VI, VII and X never came to fruition. The improved Mark II/III consisted of half-male and half-female variants. These were only intended as training tanks, but the Mark IIs ended up being shipped to France.

The key variant was the Mark IV, which was an up-armoured version of the Mark I, of which 1,220 were built comprising 420 males, 595 females and 205 tank tenders. This tank weighed 28.4 tonnes and required an eight-man crew. The male was armed with two 6-pounder guns plus three .303 Lewis machine guns, while the female was equipped with five Lewis guns. On the Mark IV and V females the sponsons were smaller being only half height top down. As with most British tanks of the time it was slow, managing just 4mph depending on the conditions. During the summer of 1917 the Mark IV fought at Messines Ridge and the Third Battle of Ypres. In November of that year 432 Mark IVs were committed to the Battle of Cambrai.

The smaller British Medium Mark A Whippet was designed to support the slow heavy tanks by exploiting any breakthroughs. The first production tanks were delivered in October 1917 from an order for 200; this was increased to 385 but later cancelled. The Whippet was directly derived from the experimental 'Little Willie' prototype. While the Whippet looks more like the tank as we know it, the crew compartment consisted of a fixed turret at the rear of the vehicle. This was armed with four machine guns, but as there were only three crew it meant that the gunner had his work cut out for him.

Efforts to improve the engine and transmission on British tanks resulted in the improved Mark V heavy tank. A number of Mark Is and IVs were fitted with various experimental transmissions, power units and clutches in February 1917 and tested by the Tank Supply Department in early March. Notably one was fitted with a epicycle gearbox that had been designed by Major Wilson. Epicycle gearing and brakes were used to replace the existing change speed gearing in the rear horns. Likewise a four-speed gearbox on the planetary principle replaced the two-speed box and worm gear. Another tank utilised the Westinghouse petrol-electric drive that was managed by one man. Also each track was given smoother variable speed control with the installation of a separate motor and generator. Another had a Daimler petrol-electric drive, while a third was fitted with Williams-Janney hydraulic pumps which gave a similar result.

The petrol-electrics had their advantages but were difficult to manufacture so it was decided to go with Wilson's epicyclic gearbox. This meant that gear changes could be conducted by the driver – providing much better handling and control. While the resulting Mark V had a hull and armament similar to the Mark IV it featured a new purpose-built Ricardo tank engine with 150hp. The Mark V also had improvements to the hull. These included a raised cupola at the rear for the commander, which gave better visibility and access to the unditching beam. Extra protection was provided by a machine gun in the rear of the hull and for signalling a semaphore arm could be erected aft of the cupola.

This improved tank went into production in December 1917 at the Metropolitan Carriage and Wagon Works, Birmingham. The Tank Corps received the very first Mark Vs in France in May 1918. Although the Mark V began to replace the Mark IV by mid-1918 many Mark IVs remained in service when the war came to a close. In total some 400 of the Mark V were built with 50:50 male to female and these first saw combat on 4 July 1918 at the Battle of Hamel.

By late 1917 it was apparent that the trench-crossing capabilities of British tanks needed to be improved. This resulted in the Tadpole Tail, which was a kit that could stretch the rear horns of a tank by nine feet. Trails showed this to be unsatisfactory. The Tank Corps Central Workshop instead came up with a field modification, by adding an extra 6ft side panelling, that extended the tank hull rather than stretching the horns. This was designated the Mark V* and it was hoped to use it as a troop carrier – this variant was tried at Amiens but the fumes gassed the occupants. As a result it was used to carry stores, by the time of the Armistice 327 had been converted and were in service with the British Army and another twenty-three were deployed with the US 301st Tank Battalion along with twelve standard Mark Vs. A factory-built variant known as the Mark V** was not available until after the war ended.

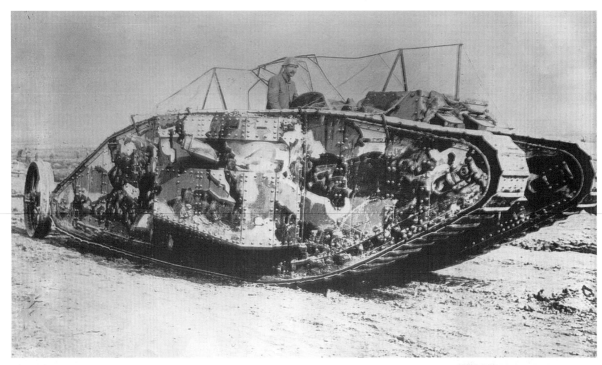

Mark I tanks were produced as male versions with 6-pounder guns mounted in their side sponsons and female versions armed with machine guns clad in armoured jackets or sleeves – seen here. This particular tank has been painted in the early Solomon camouflage scheme; its use was soon abandoned after mud made it completely unnecessary.

A British Mark I/II male tank dubbed *Lusitania*, identifiable by its long-barrelled naval 6-pounder (8 cwt 40 calibre) gun.

Access to the Mark I and subsequent models was primarily via the doors in the rear of the gun sponsons. This Mark II is fitted with the wide spudded track shoes, which clearly did not prevent it becoming stuck.

This Mark II male was photographed passing through a French village in 1917. It has baffle plates over its exhaust outlets.

Tank production was slow and the first fifty were not shipped to France until August 1916. These are Mark Vs being assembled by the Metropolitan Carriage and Wagon Company in Birmingham.

A field full of female tanks awaiting delivery.

Tanks in their storage sheds – vehicle training took place at Thetford in Norfolk.

British Vickers machine gun crew – initially the tank force was dubbed the Heavy Section Machine Gun Corps in part to keep its brand-new role secret. The Machine Gun Corps did not keep control of the tanks, the Tank Corps being created instead.

A Mark II male with spudded tracks captured by the Germans near Arras on 11 April 1917. This type of tank was only intended as a training vehicle but ended up being shipped to the front.

The subsequent Mark IV and V were armed with the shorter 6 cwt 23 calibre gun.

Mark IV male tank called *Hyacinth* temporarily stranded in captured German defences near Ribecourt in November 1917 during the Cambrai offensive.

Mark IV female with underground beam at Peronne during the German offensive in March 1918. Note the much smaller machine-gun sponson.

Mark IV Male with Tadpole Tail extension.

This Mark V* female tank is carrying a 'Crib' which replaced the brushwood fascines for trench crossing. It is traversing the Hindenburg Line in 1918 along with a mortar team.

Preserved Mark V female – this again gives a clear view of the foreshortened sponson.

Chapter Three

Heavy or Light?

Like the British tank programme the French development process was far from plain sailing. Although the French endured more teething troubles with their heavy tanks, unlike the British they refused to rush them prematurely into battle. It would not be until April 1917 and the Battle of the Chemin des Dames that the first French tank received it baptism of fire.

France had some early experience with armoured fighting vehicles. The French firm Charron-Girardot et Voigt developed the very first production armoured car in 1904, which preceded the British Rolls-Royce armoured car by a decade. It weighed three tons and featured a fully rotating turret armed with a machine gun. Although the French were not as successful as the British in developing the heavy tank concept, they did develop a highly successful light tank that impacted on post-war thinking.

Led by Colonel Jean Baptiste Estienne, the French proved even more enthusiastic about developing the tank than the British. They evolved their ideas on completely separate lines at the same time and there seems to have been little if any co-operation with the British. Estienne was serving on the Western Front with the French artillery in 1915. He was an enthusiastic advocate of new technology and as early as 1909 pioneered artillery target spotting using aircraft. Talking to other officers at the Battle of the Marne in September 1914 he commented, 'Whoever shall first be able to make land ironclads armed and equipped will have won the war'.

Like Swinton, Estienne recognized the battlefield utility of the Holt artillery tractor as a potential weapon of war. He wrote to the French CinC, General Joseph Joffre, asking to discuss with him 'mobile armoured constructions for the purpose of assuring the progress of the infantry, with a mechanical traction capable of conveying infantry through or over obstacles, under fire, with arms and baggage and with guns, at the speed of nearly 7kmh'.

Colonel Estienne was ordered to Paris to confer with the industrialist Louis Renault. He specialized in motor vehicles and did not have any experience with tracked tractors. The firm of Schneider, on the other hand, were the French representatives of the American Holt Company. They had already experimented producing a Baby Holt agricultural tractor capable of cutting through enemy barbed wire.

To mask what they were up to the French authorities set up a commission to co-ordinate tank development called the Committee for Special Artillery. This seemed to imply that the French saw the tank more as a self-propelled gun than an armoured personnel carrier. By the spring of 1916 the French companies St-Chamond and Schneider had developed what essentially were two versions of an assault gun. Indeed they were called *artillerie d'assault* and were little more than the French 75mm gun mounted forward on a Holt chassis enclosed in an armoured box.

The Schneider CA1 and St-Chamond heavy tanks were simply too cumbersome for the battlefield. The low tractor layout made them top-heavy and therefore unstable. In addition they had poor trench-crossing capabilities. The Schneider was a box-type tank, lacking a turret but with a 75mm fortress gun on the right side. It had poor mobility, was cramped and under-armed. This 13-tonne tracked box had a crew of six and could manage 5mph. Some 400 were built and they first went into action on the Chemin des Dames on 16 April 1917, suffering heavy losses.

The St-Chamond was an equally flawed design; most notably it was underpowered and the tracks were not long enough for the bulky hull. This lumbering box was armed with a larger 75mm field gun installed in the nose of the vehicle. This made it considerably longer and heavier than the Schneider. As a result the St-Chamond struggled to overcome enemy obstacles or cross trenches, becoming easily ditched or stranded. Around 400 of these 23-tonne monsters were built which could manage a maximum speed of 6mph. It was first used in combat at Laffaux Mill on 5 May 1917. Despite numerous improvements, if the war had not ended, the St-Chamond was to have been replaced by British heavy tanks.

In the meantime Estienne went back to Renault and asked them to look at developing a light close-support tank that could fight alongside the infantry. By December 1916 a model was complete but the small rotating turret was only armed with a machine gun, which caused some controversy with the Committee for Special Artillery. Nonetheless an order for 150 vehicles was placed. Successful trials in April 1917 resulted in 1,000 being purchased on the condition the tank received a heavier gun.

Orders for the FT-17 totalled 3,500 by September 1917 with Berliet, Somua and Delaunay-Belleville all called on to help build the diminutive tank. Production was not trouble-free as there were problems with the fabrication of the cast turret's armour plate. To speed production this problem was overcome by designing an octagonal turret with flat armour plates. This two-man tank, weighing just 6.5 tonnes, made its combat debut during the Second Battle of Marne on 31 May 1918. Some thirty FTs successfully broke through but lacking infantry support were obliged to withdraw.

In technical terms the FT-17 was vastly superior to the British and French heavy tanks. Unlike the heavy Schneider and St-Chamond the Renault did not have a distinct chassis; instead the running gear and the engine were mounted in the hull – a characteristic that would be maintained by the bulk of post-war tank designs. The 35bhp Renault engine was fitted in the rear and the petrol was pumped (unlike the British gravity feed) from two tanks that could hold a total of 22 gallons of fuel. Maximum speed was 4.8mph.

The transmission incorporated a Renault gearbox and cone clutches, giving the tank four forward speeds and one reverse. The engine was accessed through panels. The engine was separated from the fighting compartment by a steel bulkhead with ventilation shutters that could be closed in the event of an engine fire. The ammunition was stored along the walls of the fighting compartment and the base of the turret.

Another modern feature of the tank was access. This was through two hatches that formed the glacis plate. The driver sat below these hatches, his basic canvas seat at floor level. He controls included steering levers on either side and a gear lever on the right. Visibility was via three slots and an opening shutter. Steering was achieved by declutching and braking the transmission to the tracks on either side via the steering levers.

Unlike its heavier cousins, on the FT the tracks extended well beyond the hull. This and a removable tail to lengthen the hull enabled it to climb in and out of shell craters and trenches. The drive sprocket was at the rear and the tracks were tensioned by an adaptable front idler. At ground level the tracks ran on four sets of wheels, one of three and three of two. These were mounted on a longitudinal girder carried on leaf springs. The upper track return was borne by a rail with six small guide rollers. The rail was pivoted at the back and then tensioned upwards against the track by a coil spring at the front. The track life could easily be preserved by shipping the FT light tank to the front on trailers or trucks.

Initially the FT-17's manually-operated turret was armed with the 8mm Hotchkiss machine gun but it was soon up-gunned to take the 37mm Puteaux gun. The gunner was located in the turret where he could either sit on a small adjustable seat or stand. The turret featured a rudimentary cupola and hatch. The very prominent dome gave access and the mounting ring for this was fitted with five visions slits.

When the Americans entered the First World War in 1917 they formed a tank corps, with the heavy battalions equipped with British heavy tanks and the light battalions with the FT. American plans were ambitious, the intention was to form twenty tank battalions equipped with 1,200 US-built FTs designated the M1917 –

rising to 4,000. However, only 950 M1917s were built in America and none saw combat.

During the 1920s the FT-17 was to prove an enormous export success for France with it sold to Belgium, Brazil, China, Czechoslovakia, Finland, Holland, Japan and Poland. The Russians also built it under licence, designating it the KS (*Krasnoye Sormovo*) or 'Russki Reno', as, did the Italians as the Fiat 3000. By 1940 it was still in service with the French Army and saw action during the Second World War.

In 1914 the French Army was largely composed of infantry. Once they had dug in they, like the British, sought a way of overcoming enemy trenches.

French gunners with a Holt artillery tractor in the spring of 1915. The French firm Schneider & Co were the representatives of the American Holt Company and sought to develop a tank based on the Baby Holt agricultural tractor.

French engineers conducting a final test with a caterpillar tractor on 21 February 1916. This formed the basis of the Schneider tank design.

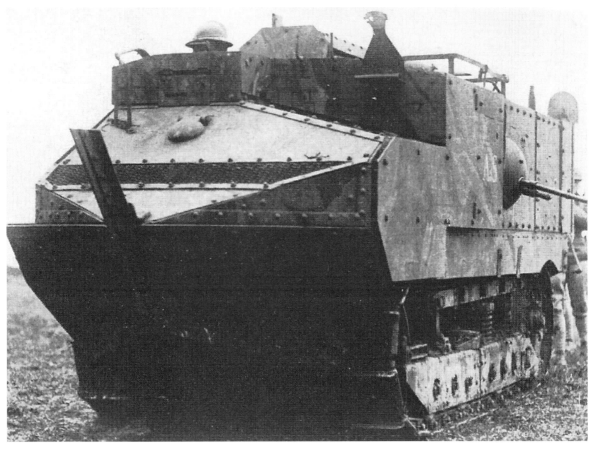

The French favoured the *char d'assaullt* concept. This resulted in the Schneider CA1 of which around 400 were built. It first went into action in April 1917 and suffered heavy losses.

Much more successful was the Renault FT-17 light tank. Like British tanks it had an all-round track layout that prevented it becoming ditched.

St-Chamond also came up with a box-type tank armed with a M1897 75mm field gun mounted in the nose. The body was much too big for the tracks and it struggled to traverse enemy trenches without getting stuck.

A number of different FT-17 variants were built – the initial *char mitrailleuse* model was armed with the 8mm Hotchkiss machine gun. However, the French Committee for Special Artillery insisted that it be up-gunned.

The subsequent *char cannon* FT-17 model had the short 37mm Puteaux SA gun. This type constitutes about a third of FT-17s built.

The Renault FT 75 BS was an early self-propelled gun model featuring a larger turret to house a short-barrel Blockhaus Schneider 75mm gun. Very few of these were actually built.

The Americans sought to licence-build the FT-17 as the M1917 to equip the American Expeditionary Force (AEF), but none were produced in time to see action. The AEF had to rely on tanks supplied by the British and French instead.

The AEF was expecting 300 M1917s by April 1918. In the event just two arrived in France on 20 November 1918, nine days after the end of the war.

French workers put the finishing touches to a St-Chamond tank. This was essentially a self-propelled assault gun.

While the Schneider tank was a slightly better design than the St-Chamond, it suffered from the same design faults.

Chapter Four

First Blood at Flers

By the summer of 1916 General Sir Douglas Haig, CinC British Expeditionary Force, needed to draw German pressure off the beleaguered French at Verdun. To do this Haig was forced to commit the new and raw divisions of Kitchener's Army to an attack along the Somme Valley. Launched on 1 July 1916, the Somme offensive saw the British Army mown down. On the very first day British troops suffered almost 60,000 casualties. The first phase of the offensive was brought to a halt on the wire before the German trenches, so Haig called for the tanks to be committed at the earliest opportunity.

There is no question that the tank was a revolutionary weapon. Whilst the generals appreciated that it needed a local battlefield trial, to have done this would have risked losing the element of surprise. It would also permit the Germans to prepare countermeasures should they capture one. Just before renewing the battle Haig wrote to General Sir William Robertson, Chief of the Imperial General Staff, 'Even if I do not get as many as I hope, I shall use what I have got, as I cannot wait any longer for them, and it would be folly not to use any means at my disposal in what is likely to be our crowning effort for this year'. At the time of the British offensive of the 150 tanks built only sixty had been shipped to France, of which forty-nine were committed to battle.

Winston Churchill was 'shocked at the proposal to expose this tremendous secret to the enemy upon such a petty scale and as a mere make-weight to what I was sure could only be an indecisive operation'. The future of the tank now unfairly hung on its performance at the Somme. Historians have since been divided over whether Haig should have waited longer before unleashing the tank. The military historian Alistair Horne wrote 'All warnings and entreaties from inventors, sponsors, and Cabinet ministers not to use the first few untried vehicles prematurely, not to throw away their secret before there were enough to be launched into a mass assault on the German trenches, were ruthlessly disregarded'. In contrast, the respected First World War historian Hew Strachan says 'The argument that the British had forfeited their surprise value by using them prematurely on the Somme in September 1916 is nonsense: here was an imperfect but evolving weapon which needed the benefit of combat experience.'

Colonel (latter Major-General Sir) Ernest Swinton, appointed chief of the Heavy Section, Machine Gun Corps in March 1916, intended to form three whole tank battalions – each of five companies with twelve tanks each. GHQ vetoed this, calling for a basic company organization, each with twenty-five tanks. By the time of the very first tank action at Flers-Courcelette six tank companies had been formed, designated A to F – of these C and D arrived in France in August, A in September on the morning of the attack and B in October. By the time of the Battle of Amiens in August 1918 they had been expanded to eighteen battalions, sixteen of which were deployed in France with more in the process of forming.

General Sir Henry Rawlinson, commanding the British 4th Army, was sceptical about the tank. Just a fortnight before the battle, on 29 August, he informed King George V's assistant private secretary:

> We are puzzling our heads as to how best to make use of them and have not yet come to a decision. They are not going to take the British Army straight to Berlin as some people imagine but if properly used and skilfully handled by the detachments who work them they may prove very useful in taking trenches and strongpoints. Some people are rather too optimistic as to what these weapons will accomplish.

For no apparent reason, and without reference to Swinton, Haig decided to spread his tanks in penny packets across an entire three corps front: on the right and centre right seventeen tanks were each allocated to 14th and 15th Corps, eight to 3rd Corps in the centre while the remaining seven were held with the Reserve Army. Just before the attack the tanks had moved up by train, to an area near Bray-sur-Somme called 'The Loop' and on 13 September they deployed to their assembly areas. In particular D company drove to 'Green Dump' behind Delville Wood to the west of Ginchy.

It took them nine frustrating hours to cover the three miles to the front line. Lieutenant Arnold commanding D16 feared they would not reach their 'jump off' position in time and was on the verge of sending out his carrier pigeon with a warning. Luckily D16 clanked into position just as the infantry were climbing from their trenches.

For the next phase of the Battle of the Somme on 15 September 1916 just forty-nine Mark Is were available to spearhead the assault of Rawlinson's 4th Army. There was no element of strategic surprise as Rawlinson preceded his attack with a three-day bombardment of German positions employing 1,250 guns (one gun for every three yards). The inexperienced tank crews rumbled into No Man's Land with instructions to break through the enemy lines. Only thirty-six crossed the start line and many of the others became disabled or stranded in the wastes of No Man's Land. Massive shell craters and ditches proved major obstacles.

Lieutenant Stuart Henderson Hastie, commanding D17, was tasked along with D9 and D14 with taking Flers in the German centre. They were ordered to first silence German machine guns on the Tea Trench Line and await the infantry. After this they were to push on the Switch Trench Line and through the Flers defences. The crew of D17 soon found themselves on their own as the other two tanks became stuck in a sunken road. D17's tail wheels were soon but out of action, which meant steering had to be by using the brakes and that put a great strain on the Daimler engine.

Gunner A. H. R. Reiffer, MM, wrote 'I was No.2 gunner to Percy Boult on the starboard 6-pounder gun and our day started when Boult excitedly told me he was going to fire at a German observation balloon (spotting for the artillery). Several rounds were fired and Boult claimed a direct hit. The balloon disappeared and this may have had some bearing on the partial success of the tanks attacking Flers.'

They managed to reach the ruins of Flers and silenced several German machine guns firing from the remains of some houses. At the village crossroads they came under fire from a German field gun battery but managed to trundle up the main street of Flers. At this point a runner reached them with orders to retire as they were at risk of being hit by their own artillery. Very slowly D17 withdrew to a ridge in front of Delville Wood where the struggling engine finally packed up for good. Hastie left to consult with Lieutenant Head, another tank commander. It was then that a German barrage hit D17, wrecking one of the tracks. Corporal Shelson instructed the crew to abandon the tank and take shelter in Head's vehicle.

In Britain Flers was trumpeted as a great success, with one headline reading 'A tank is walking up the High Street of Flers with the British Army cheering behind!' It later transpired of the ten tanks allotted to the 41st Division in the centre of 15th Corps' sector only D6, D16 and D17 managed to reach the vicinity of Flers.

A review of the Mark I's performance on the Somme showed it had been useful but little more. The hasty preparations and mechanical defects meant that just over thirty tanks reached the start line. Of these just nine accompanied the infantry, nine failed to catch up but assisted clearing overrun enemy positions, nine broke down and nine became 'ditched' in the craters. Only the first nine helped redeem in a very limited way the failure of the Somme offensive by taking Flers. Where they did break through singularly or in groups they enjoyed some tactical success. After the first day of fighting, few of the tanks were in a fit state to carry on.

While Haig and Rawlinson's use of tanks at Flers was hardly an unparalleled success it showed what could be achieved. Allowances needed to be made for the conditions the tanks had to fight in and the inexperience of the new crews. In addition the generals had spread those tanks available far too thinly across a very wide front. Nonetheless, greatly encouraged, Haig noted, 'Wherever the tanks advanced we took our objectives and where they did not advance were did not take our objectives'.

It was 15th Corps that had the most success and marked the tanks' first triumph in taking the village of Flers. There can be no denying the courage of Lieutenant Stuart Hastie and his crew at Flers. They achieved their objectives and successfully engaged the enemy. Hastie was awarded the Military Cross and his citation read 'For conspicuous gallantry in action. He fought his tank with great gallantry, reaching the third objective. Later he rendered valuable service in salving a tank lying out under very heavy fire.'

In contrast 14th Corps was obstructed by the German defensive position known as the 'Quadrilateral'. Its tanks got lost and at least one accidentally headed for the British lines, firing on its own troops. This reportedly happened in other corps' sectors. The Canadian 2nd Division from Gough's Reserve Army (later the 5th Army), on the extreme left of the main attack, successfully moved up the Bapaume road and captured Courcelette. However, their allocation of tanks struggled to keep up with the infantry.

Whilst the 15th (Scottish) Division took Martinpuich it ended up supported by one surviving tank that helped clear trenches. The 50th Northumbrian Division were held up by enemy machine guns in the High Wood. This was because the 47th (London) Division took several hours to clear the woods, with its three surviving tanks proving a hindrance amongst the tree stumps. The delay limited much of 3rd Corps advance and they did not reach the German third line.

Basil Liddell Hart in his History of the First World War was dismissive of the handing of the tank's inauspicious debut, writing 'Their early employment before large numbers were ready was a mistake; losing the chance of a great strategic surprise, and owing also to tactical mishandling, and minor technical defects they had only limited success.'

Overall the tank operation had been a failure. Perhaps the generals should not be blamed for being so eager to rush their new weapon into battle, as they would have been remiss if they had not called on every available means at the Somme. Cold statistics though showed that any strategic punch the tank could have offered if the tankers had been given more time to prepare was thrown away.

Nonetheless Haig and his generals were prepared to give the tank a second chance. He requested that 1,000 tanks be built for 1917 and on 8 October 1916 supported the creation of the Tank Corps. Colonel Hugh Elles who had been with the tanks from the start was appointed commander and the brilliant if somewhat temperamental Major J. F. C Fuller was chief of staff. These two men ensured the new Tank Corps was given a highly competent foundation.

They recruited veterans who understood conditions on the Western Front. Experience on the Somme showed that the crews needed special overalls, gauntlets and reinforced leather helmets. The standard British Army helmet with its broad brim was found to be too wide and tended to snag inside the tank. The new leather helmet was fitted with a visor to guard against 'splash' – metal splinters which showered the interior of the tank after it was hit.

Despite Haig's support, certain senior elements tried to throttle the tank programme. Lloyd George was displeased to discover that General Robertson, the Chief of the Imperial General Staff, had countermanded his order for 1,000 tanks. He recalled, 'I discovered this countermand in time, and gave peremptory instructions that the manufacture should be proceeded with and that the utmost diligence should be used in executing the order'. Although Lloyd George supported the war, he sometimes had a troubled relationship with the generals. They regarded him as militarily naive while he did not altogether trust their motives. Seeking a way out of the impasse on the Western Front, Lloyd George suggested distracting the enemy by diverting forces to Italy or Salonika. Robertson and Haig, who did not want to divert resources from what they saw as the main theatre of operations, opposed this proposal. Lloyd George found himself stuck with them throughout the war.

Nonetheless, Haig's request for such a massive armoured force was seen as a clear vindication of the tank advocates. Lieutenant Stern, promoted to Major in charge of the newly-constituted Tank Supply Department, set to work. A new design was needed to remedy the Mark I's shortcomings, but in the meantime 100 interim models designated the Mark II and III were built. The improvements were fairly limited, consisting of a revised hatch and raised conning tower on top of the hull and wider spudded track shoes on every sixth link for better traction. The Mark III also had thicker armour that would become standard on the Mark IV. These two interim models, with fifty of each being built, were deployed to support the Mark Is as training tanks. Much to Stern's alarm the Mark IIs saw action at Arras, Messines and Ypres. Although some were used at Cambrai in November 1917 most had been replaced by the newer Mark IV by then.

The improved Mark IV was ready to go into production by February 1917. It retained the rhomboidal shape of its predecessors, but was enhanced by thicker armour, two shorter 6-pounders and was the first tank to carry the excellent Lewis machine gun. The latter was eventually replaced by French Hotchkiss machine gun. By this stage the Germans had developed an anti-tank rifle that could penetrate the sides of the Mark I so the armour on the Mark IV was increased to 12mm. The 28-ton male was 26ft 5in long, 12ft 9in wide and 8ft 2in high. It had a trench-crossing capability of 10ft but like its predecessors could only crawl along at a cripplingly slow 3.7 mph.

The main problem with the Mark I design was the unsatisfactory Daimler engine and the transmission. Frustratingly the Mark IV used the same engine and transmission as the earlier models, but featured an external fuel tank with an Autovac pump between the rear horns as well as silencer and exhaust pipe for the engine. It also had smaller gun sponsons, that could be swung inward for transportation, and, with the shorter 6-pounder guns, this assisted with manoeuvrability and clearance.

Once superseded by the newer models the Mark I to IIIs were either used for special-purpose roles or training. Some were converted to Supply Tanks by having their guns removed and the embrasures plated over. These could carry supplies as well as tow field 'tank sledges' built by the Tank Corps Central Workshops in France. These sledges could shift up to 10 tons of stores with the Supply Tanks capable of towing up to three at a time. Redundant Mark Is were also used as command or wireless tanks. One unarmed sponson was converted to carry wireless equipment while the other served as a field office. These were first deployed at Cambrai and this was the first time tanks were used in combat as wireless platforms.

On 1 July 1916 the British CinC in France General Sir Douglas Haig launched an offensive on the Somme to alleviate pressure on the French at Verdun. The first phase failed so his new tanks were called on to break through.

Opposite left: German infantry in their distinctive leather *Pickelhaube* helmets. From 1916 onwards this was replaced by the *Stahlhelm* or steel helmet, this provided some protection not only from shrapnel but also during brutal hand-to-hand fighting in the trenches.

British infantry moving up during the Battle of the Somme. On the first day of the offensive the British Army suffered 60,000 casualties.

British wounded and a German PoW at Bernafay Wood on 19 July 1916. The Somme became a byword for slaughter.

General Sir Henry Rawlinson, commanding the British 4th Army, was highly sceptical about the decisive impact expected of the tank during the renewed Battle of the Somme.

A Mark I male tank with its distinctive wheeled steering tail and chicken-wire 'bomb roof'. Both features were dropped on the later models of tank. A camouflage scheme is visible on both the rear and front horns. The Mark I made its combat debut during the Battle of Flers-Courcelette.

A Mark I male on the Somme on 25 September 1916. Just forty-nine tanks were available for the renewal of the offensive ten days earlier. The mud has blotted out the tank's Solomon camouflage.

Infantry moving up past a damaged and abandoned Mark I during the Flers-Courcelette attack.

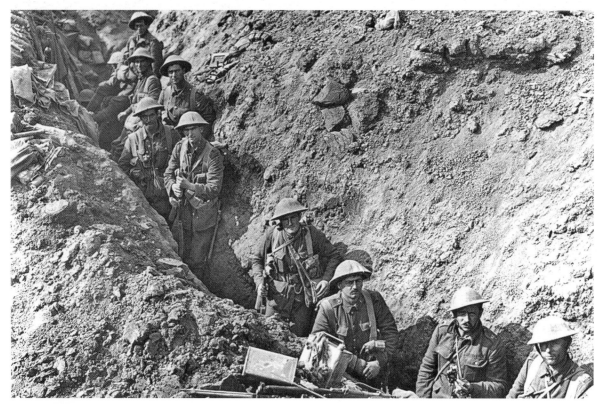

Men of the New Zealand Division in the Switch Line near Flers in September 1916.

Commanded by Captain Inglis, C5 *Crème de Menthe* was damaged by artillery fire during the fighting on Pozières Ridge. One of the tail wheels has been blown off.

The King of Belgium inspects one of the Mark Is involved in the Flers-Courcelette operation.

Men on the exposed road to Pozières in August 1916.

A British female tank with a captured camouflaged German gun. British painter Solomon Joseph Solomon argued that it was impossible to effectively camouflage a tank because of its large shadow. He reasoned that netting would produce better results and net production was increased in 1917.

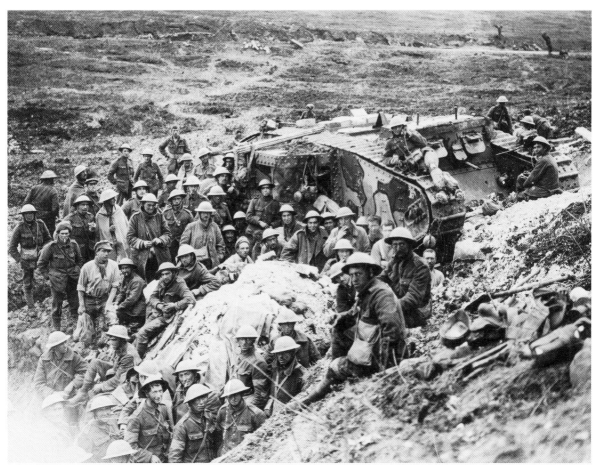

British troops gathered round a Mark I two days after the Flers-Courcelette fighting. It is clearly sporting the early camouflage scheme on the front horns.

Chapter Five

French Heavies at Berry-au-Bac

In late 1916 General Robert Nivelle was appointed French Commander-in-Chief. The following spring he was optimistically arguing that a breakthrough and victory was possible. He proposed an offensive east of Paris on the Aisne River between Soissons and Reims toward the heavily fortified Chemin des Dames ridge. Haig reluctantly agreed to conduct a diversionary assault way to the north at Arras to tie down the German reserves. The intention was that the British and French offensives would coincide with attacks on the Russian and Italian fronts. However, the Russians were exhausted and in the throes of revolution while the Italians were not ready.

Some seven months after the British first blooded their tanks at Flers-Courcelette the French Army decided to do likewise. By 1 April 1917 over 200 Schneider CA1 heavy tanks had been delivered to the front. Unfortunately they were without their self-starters and the lack of spares immobilized over thirty of them immediately. As part of the Nivelle offensive the plan was that 132 Schneiders organized into eight companies and deployed in two battle groups would strike north-west from Berry-au-Bac towards the plain between the Aisne River at Neufchâtel and Soissons.

Nivelle proposed that just after the British attack at Arras three French armies would strike on the Aisne, secure the Chemin des Dames ridge and cut through German defences toward Laon to threaten the railway network supporting the German front. However, Nivelle's preparations were disrupted when the Germans withdrew from the Somme to the newly-built concrete fortifications of the Hindenburg Line. This greatly straightened the German line between Arras and Soissons and caused problems for the French 3rd Army.

Unfortunately the Germans captured a copy of Nivelle's plan on 4 April 1917, which had stupidly been taken into a forward position. The German defensive positions along the Chemin des Dames and into the Soissonais region were already held in depth, but now they knew the French schedule and objectives. Despite this and the German withdrawal Nivelle insisted on pressing ahead with his assault. Many senior French commanders could not see the point of this, especially in light of the German withdrawal to the Hindenburg Line.

The French generals knew that their untried tanks would not have an easy time of it. The Chemin des Dames formed part of the Hunding Line, running from Craonne to Verdun. They had good tactical intelligence of the area after German defences on the Chemin des Dames were extensively mapped at the end of February 1917. The slopes of the ridge were protected by a series of interlocking trench lines reinforced by blockhouses screened by thick belts of barbed wire. The crest of the ridge was honeycombed with tunnels and dotted in concrete pillboxes and concealed gun positions.

The British attack at Arras was launched on 9 April and as in previous engagements the tanks were misused. Just sixty were available to support the British 3rd Army's three corps and the Canadian Corps. The latter deployed to the north were tasked with taking the heavily defended Vimy Ridge. In light of Monchy-le-Preux to the south-east of Arras being the key enemy position it would have made sense to allocate the tanks to 6th Corps, but instead they were spread over the entire front. The tank force consisted of fifteen Mark Is and forty-five Mark IIs. The latter had been intended as a training tank so was not really suitable for combat. German armour-piercing bullets could penetrate both types of tank, which meant German infantry could defend themselves without relying on artillery support.

On the first day the infantry made good progress and in less than an hour captured all of the German first-line trenches. Again an opportunity was lost because the tanks were not concentrated on the south side of the salient created that day. It was only on the morning of 11 April that four tanks assisted a battalion of the 37th Division to take Monchy-le-Preux. This wedge though was too late and too narrow.

That same day Gough's 5th Army launch an attack from the south against the Hindenburg Line in an effort to draw some of the pressure off 3rd Army. It found itself rapidly advancing over the area evacuated by the Germans thereby leaving its artillery far behind. The 4th Australian Division, led by eleven tanks acting as mobile artillery and wire-cutters, struck toward Bullecourt. Although the tanks lagged behind the Australians did break into the Hindenburg Line and were soon subjected to fierce German counter-attacks. Australian confidence in the newfangled tanks was severely shaken. Tough German resistance also prevented the 3rd and 5th Armies linking up. However, Arras did achieve its principal objective, forcing the Germans to double their strength in the area within a week.

To the south, after ten days of preliminary bombardment the Germans were expecting the French infantry when they went over the top on 16 April 1917. Two groups of supporting French tanks were led by *Chef d'Escadron* Louis Bossut in the middle (this was the main force with eighty-one Schneider tanks) and by Captain Chaubes in the west. Improbably Bossut's tanks were expected to reach Provais some 5.5 miles away across four lines of enemy defences. German troops had increased the depth of their defences and the French guns ranged far too ahead of their own infantry. Possibly in anticipation of a tank attack and as a result of experience at Flers and subsequent British tank operations, the Germans had also widened their trenches and concentrated their artillery.

At Flers the British tanks had been moved up to their jump-off points at night, but at Berry-au-Bac the French made a daylight approach. Bossut was not happy about this but there was little he could do. His tank bearing the name *Trompe-la-Mort* ('Cheat death') and flying his personal pennant bearing the motto '*À fond et jusqu'au bout*' ('All the way') set off at 0630 on the 16th. His force crossed the start line at 0800 and he continually strode between the tanks urging on the crews. German spotter aircraft and artillery observation posts were soon directing artillery fire down onto the Schneiders.

The Schneider CA1 had a nasty tendency to burn because its thinly protected fuel tanks were high up on each side. Even machine-gun fire could ignite them. At Berry-au-Bac and Juvincourt the French tanks carried a lot of extra petrol because Nivelle wanted them to breakthrough on the first day and inevitably some ended up catching fire.

After forty-five minutes Bossut's tanks crossed the first German defensive line. At about 1100, as they were approaching the second German line, Bossut clambered back into his tank. By a cruel quirk of fate at that moment a German artillery shell pierced the roof and killed all six crew. Bossut's brother, who was a warrant officer in the same unit, recovered his body that night.

Despite Bossut's loss the tanks pressed on with their attack through the Germans Nassau and Wurtzburg trench lines toward the village of Prouvais. The ground had been so badly torn up by the French bombardment that the infantry could not follow. The Schneider CA1 tanks, deployed for the very first time, quickly broke down or became stuck. Bossut's force lost most of its tanks and the crews suffered 180 casualties. By the close of the first day of the 132 heavy tanks committed sixty-four had ditched and fifty-seven had been destroyed.

In early May the Schneiders were used to support the successful capture of Moulin-de-Laffaux hill. The tanks attacked with a battalion of infantry supported by a spotter plane, whose job was to pinpoint German batteries and call in counter-battery fire. Once again reliability proved a problem. Most of the tanks broke down and were left behind by the advancing infantry. Nonetheless, the hill was secured, in contrast most of the unsupported infantry attacks on Chemin des Dames ended in failure.

The French Army struggled on until the offensive had completely stalled by 9 May. Although France's first tank attack had been a partial success the Nivelle offensive was a disaster. It deployed more than double the number of tanks the British had at the Somme and lost 121 in the process – although some were salvageable. The French Army suffered 120,000 casualties securing just 600 yards of territory and 28,000 German prisoners. Ironically the French ended up gaining more ground thanks to the voluntary German withdrawal to the Hindenburg Line than from the Nivelle Offensive. Nivelle, his reputation in tatters, was replaced two weeks later.

Following the Nivelle Offensive the French Army fell into chaos and widespread mutiny. The troops said they would defend France but would not take part in any further futile offensives. The unrest started in late April and gathered pace the following month, peaking in June with some sixty-eight divisions being affected. The fiasco at the Chemin des Dames was not entirely to blame for the mutinies, to be fair Nivelle's setback represented the culmination of a process that had started in 1914. It took until the summer to restore order. In the meantime Britain was forced to assume sole responsibility for offensive operations.

Schneider CA1 heavy tanks being offloaded from rail cars. The barbette holding the short 75mm Blockhaus Schneider gun on the front right corner is visible on the two closest vehicles. Eight companies of this tank were gathered to take part on the Nivelle Offensive launched on 16 April 1917.

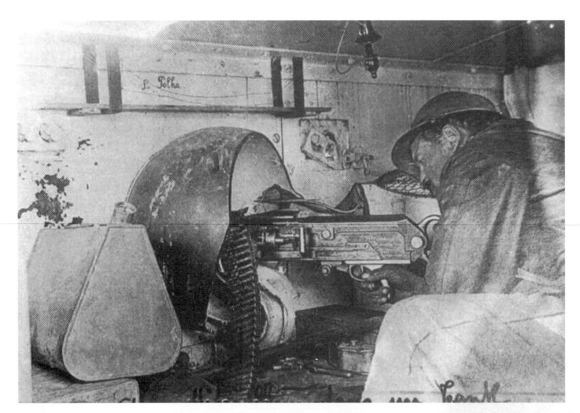

Schneider tank gunner manning one of two Hotchkiss M1814 machine guns mounted on either side in large hemispherical ball mounts.

French *Poilus*, as their soldiers were known, watching German troop movements. The German withdrawal to the Hindeburg Line made the Nivelle Offensive a largely pointless exercise. The French Adrian helmet introduced in the autumn of 1915 was the very first steel helmet issued to troops of any army during the First World War. It offered some protection against shrapnel.

The ruined village of Soupir south of the Chemin des Dames. This was the type of landscape Nivelle's tanks had to contend with.

French infantry advancing on the German's heavily-fortified positions on the Chemin des Dames ridge. The Germans did not give up this high ground easily.

By the end of the first day of the Nivelle Offensive fifty-seven Schneider CAIs had been destroyed and another sixty-four were stranded. These particular tanks were caught in the open by German artillery.

This German rifleman is sheltering by one of the Schneiders lost during the fighting at Berry-au-Bac.

The St-Chamond tank first saw combat on 5 May 1917 at Laffaux Mill. Just sixteen were committed and some broke down, others became ditched and three were destroyed by enemy fire.

French troops searching captured German positions. The infantry attacks on the Chemin de Dames largely ended in failure.

Poilus taking cover while a St-Chamond tank shells German positions. This type was even more unwieldy than the Schneider CA1.

French infantrymen displaying their battered standard in July 1917. Their weary expressions say it all. The failure of the Nivelle Offensive and heavy casualties sparked widespread mutiny amongst the exhausted French Army.

During the war a total of twelve units were formed using the St-Chamond which were designated *Artillerie Spécial* Nos 31–42. They continued to see action up until the end of the conflict.

Chapter Six

Trapped at Passchendaele

The failure of the tanks at Passchendaele was to prove an embarrassment to everyone involved. The Third Battle of Ypres, fought in the second half of 1917, was the only prolonged offensive that had true strategic ambitions. Even so Prime Minister David Lloyd George, tired of the lack of progress earlier in the year, attempted to oppose this operation. However, his ideas for transferring troops to Italy found no favour with the senior military leadership. Robertson permitted Haig to go ahead with the planned offensive and Lloyd George had to give way.

Haig hoped to take the high ground around the Ypres Salient and then liberate the Belgian Channel ports. The latter, used as German destroyer and submarine bases, had been a thorn in Britain's side since 1915. A highly ambitious amphibious landing behind the German lines was to involve tanks. The 1st Division in Rawlinson's 4th Army was assigned the assault-landing role and the tanks were to assist storming the concrete sea walls.

Lieutenant Mark Dillon, B Battalion, Tank Corps, was involved in rehearsals using a mock sea wall at Erin. He recalled: 'The tank was provided with a wooden framework or crib, which it pushed in front of it up the slope. The tank got a grip on the slope, which it normally couldn't have done, because it had fixed to its tracks slabs of wood with steel spikes in them. These steel spikes dug into the cement and enabled the tank to crawl up . . . So it proved perfectly possible to surmount those concrete coastal defences in that manner.' It was anticipated that the coastal assault would be conducted in conjunction with an attack along the coast from the Yser bridgehead. But when the Germans took the bridgehead on 10 July the landings were called off.

The Ypres offensive opened well with the storming of Messines Ridge on 7 June following the detonation of a series of mines under the German defences. The three corps of General Sir Herbert Plumer's 2nd Army were supported by a limited number of tanks. There were twenty Mark IVs assigned to the 2nd Anzac Corps, sixteen with 9th Corps, twelve with 10th Corps and twenty-four in reserve.

During the opening advance many of the tanks broke down or ditched, those that remained operational were soon outstripped by the infantry. A few caught up and at Fanny's Farm a tank burst into a German strongpoint causing the 100-strong garrison to panic and surrender. Two tanks also helped the 36th (Ulster) Division advance to the right of Wytschaete village. Mid-morning the tank reserve was thrown into the fight, joining the 2nd Anzac Corps and 9th Corps on the flanks. Those tanks that survived from the 10th Corps attack also operated from Damm and Denys Wood.

However, prolonged delays in renewing the offensive until late July gave the Germans plenty of time to strengthen their defences in front of Passchendaele Ridge. Attacking from the northern sector the British had to get over the Yser Canal, but luckily it was discovered the Germans had withdrawn from the area and by 28 July the eastern bank was secured. The British attack three days later was to involve the largest tank operation yet attempted. Unfortunately the appalling quagmire of the Ypres Salient was far from ideal tank country.

In reality Haig had once more been let down by tank production rates and had less than 150 available. He initially considered a surprise attack in the centre using tanks without artillery preparation to capture the high ground. This idea had withered thanks to the lack of tanks and the continued dislike of them in some quarters of the army. It meant, as always, that it would be up to the artillery and infantry to carry the day.

The sheer weight of the bombardment at Passchendaele rendered an already torn battlefield almost completely impassable to the tanks. It opened on 22 July and continued until 0350 on the 31st. British artillery strength totalled over 3,000 guns of which almost 1,000 were heavies. They delivered four and a quarter million shells, equating to four and three-quarter tons dropped onto every yard of the front. This was four times the number of shells fired in preparation for the Somme offensive the previous year.

To add to the tankers' problems they were not permitted to use the roads as their slow-moving vehicles chewed up the surfaces. 'The main problem was finding somewhere where you wouldn't get ditched [stuck] on your way to the line', recalled Lieutenant Dillon '. . . So you had to find a route which enabled you to waddle along and get into your position without ditching, disrupting the roads or upsetting other people who were also fighting the war – such as gunners and signallers.'

The Reverend Maurice Murray, 12th and 13th Battalions Royal Sussex Regiment, observed the tanks moving up the line:

I saw 12 huge tanks crawling away out of the wood where they had been so well hidden, that we had not seen them. The officers in charge each looked like boys and the men inside were looking out of the flaps and joking with everybody. They all seemed to be Scots. This was the first tank I had seen. Their line to the front has been taped with very broad tape and they are not to keep to the roads but go all across the marsh. These are the tanks which are to go over with us behind them tomorrow.

In places the partially-drained Yser Canal was filled with sandbags to allow the tanks to cross. Two tank battalions transited at the same point and got beyond Zillebeke Lake before they were met by German shelling. Private Reginald Beall with A Battalion remembered, 'We realised that we were in for a very serious time by the complaints the other members of the crew made that it was not to be compared with the experiences they had on the Somme – the Somme was far easier – so I guessed it must be pretty savage.'

The tanks were able to do very little to support the infantry. The mud proved to be as much a threat as the German artillery. They constantly got stuck in the boggy ground and many had to be abandoned, especially if they started to sink. On the right the attack against the Gheluvelt Ridge faltered and tank losses were heavy. The 2nd Tank Brigade deployed forty-eight tanks in front of 2nd Corps, but just nineteen managed to get into action and all but one became a casualty. The initial offensive petered out by 3 August far short of its objectives. In those four days the Allies suffered 35,000 casualties.

Two weeks later the British offensive was resumed with attacks on Langemarck and the Gheluvelt plateau. There occurred a minor triumph in infantry-tank co-operation on 19 August 1917 when an operation was conducted to take some fortified farms beyond St Julien. A composite tank company was put together under Major R. H. Broome with orders to move up the St Julien-Poelcappelle road to attack troublesome enemy pillboxes from behind. Although the road was in ruins like everywhere else, crucially it offered firmer going for the tanks. This was important if any real progress was to be made.

Machine-gun fire and aircraft were to mask the noise of the tanks getting to their jump-off positions. On the approach the tanks were to be covered by smoke and a shrapnel barrage. At 0445 eleven tanks set off but four broke down or got stuck. Nonetheless Hillock Farm was occupied at 0600 and fifteen minutes later male G29 and female G32 approached the Maison de Hibou pillbox. Supported by machine-gun fire from the female tank, G29 under Second Lieutenant A. G. Barker fired forty rounds from its 6-pounders into the two back entrances of the strongpoint. In response sixty German infantry ran out, half of whom were captured. Barker's tank then got stuck but its right-hand gun continued firing, deliver twenty rounds into enemy positions until the sinking tank had to be abandoned.

Two tanks also attacked the Cockcroft pillbox, but the male tank developed engine trouble and fumes rendered six of the crew unconscious. The wounded commander and the driver managed to get back to St Julien before getting ditched.

The other tank gunned down many of the German garrison when they tried to flee their position. It also got stuck so its commander, Second Lieutenant H. Coutts, sent a pigeon and two crew to summon the infantry to consolidate Cockcroft. After this successful operation five of the seven tanks got back safely.

Lieutenant Mark Dillon, B Battalion, Tank Corps wrote of this action:

It is important, because at the time there was a very strong anti-tank lobby at headquarters. Haig and the cavalry generals were all terrified that they would lose their horses and they were trying at home and at GHQ to have the tanks abolished. Now this just turned the tide and using that little battle as a lever our tank headquarters were able to persuade GHQ to try a bigger attack on exactly the same principles – that is to say sticking to hard going where it hasn't been knocked about by shellfire, going in without artillery preparation to get surprise and to have close co-operation with the infantry. And that was what led to the battle of Cambrai.

On 20 September General Hubert Plumer's 2nd Army relaunched the offensive on the Menin Road with subsequent attacks on Polygon Wood and Broodseinde Ridge. This time the ground was firm enough for the tanks to move forward. German resistance was fierce. Some seventeen tanks were lost at Clapham Junction, on the Menin Road 1.25 miles east of Ypres, gaining it the name 'the tank graveyard'. On 4 October the rains returned and by the autumn both sides had fought each other to a standstill – though the fighting went on.

Then on 23 October 1917 it was the turn of the French when eight divisions renewed the attack on the Chemin des Dames Ridge. They were supported by Schneider and St-Chamond heavy tanks that moved forward to engage enemy positions missed by the six-day preliminary bombardment. This time things went better than in April at Berry-au-Bac. When the French infantry dug in around the remains of Fort de la Malmaison on top of the ridge the tanks helped protect them from German counter-attacks. The hard-won foothold on the shell-swept plateau cost the French army 14,000 casualties, but the demoralized Germans lost 38,000 killed, wounded or missing and 12,000 captured.

At Ypres the British finally called it a day on 12 November. Lloyd George described Passchendaele as 'the battle which, with the Somme and Verdun, will always rank as the most gigantic, tenacious, grim, futile and bloody fight ever waged in the history of war'. By this point the Third Battle of Ypres had cost British and Commonwealth forces 70,000 dead with another 200,000 wounded or captured. The tank had still not achieved decisive results for either the British or French armies. Despite its failure at Passchendaele the Tank Corps' faith in their new steeds remained unshaken.

The British Army's most senior officer, General Sir William Robertson, Chief of the Imperial General Staff, tried to stifle Lloyd George and Haig's enthusiasm for the tank. Nonetheless he supported Haig's commitment of tanks to the Battles of Messines and Passchendaele in the summer of 1917.

This aerial photo was taken over Messines on 2 June 1917. The lunar landscape is peppered with shell craters as far as the eye can see. Seven days later nineteen enormous British mines devastated the German front lines, killing around 10,000 men.

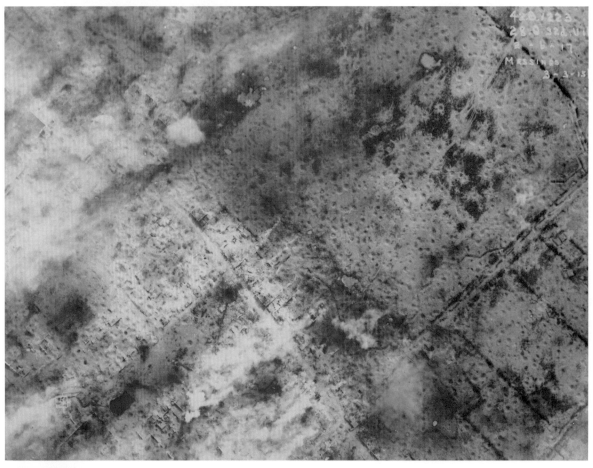

Some of the soldiers killed by the British mines on Messines Ridge.

British tanks moving up for the attack. Just seventy tanks were available for the opening stages of the Third Battle of Ypres known as the Battle of Messines.

A massive British 15in howitzer. The bombardment at Passchendaele tore up the battlefield even more, and added to this the rain made the ground all but impassable for the tanks.

British 18-pounder battery near Boesinghe on 31 July 1917.

This is what greeted the tank crews – a morass of boggy ground that would suck the unwary under.

This tank lost its tracks and was destroyed by German shell fire.

Stranded in a sea of mud and craters. Passchendaele proved wholly unsuitable for the deployment of tanks. Only along the firmer ground of the St Julien-Poelcappelle road did they achieve any notable success.

The Third Battle of Ypres was re-launched on 20 September 1917 on the Menin Road. These wounded Australians were photographed on the Menin Road, near Birr Cross that day.

Two abandoned tanks at 'the tank graveyard' near Clapham Junction east of Ypres looking toward Sanctuary Wood on 23 September 1917.

18-pounders belonging to the Australian 2nd Division near Bellewaarde Lake, Ypres, in action on 28 September 1917.

The French renewed their attack on the Chemin des Dames Ridge on 23 October 1917 employing their St-Chamond (seen here) and Schneider tanks. This time they achieved better results than during the ill-fated Nivelle Offensive in April.

Men from the Australian 4th Division amidst the shattered remains of Chäteau Wood near Hooge in the Ypres Salient at the end of October 1917. Men, animals and vehicles were simply swallowed by the deep mud.

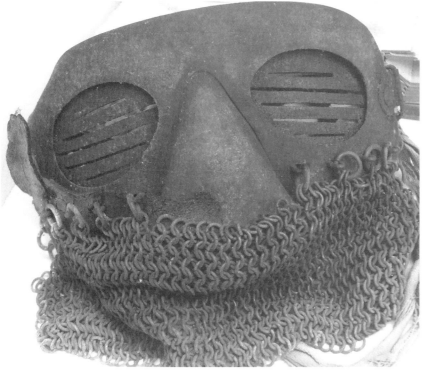

The rather sinister-looking 'splatter mask' which formed part of the British leather and chain-mail tank helmet designed to protect the wearer's face and head inside the tank.

Chapter Seven

Fortress Cambrai

It was not until November 1917 and the Battle of Cambrai that Elles and Fuller were finally permitted to deploy the Tank Corps en masse in line with their evolving tactical doctrine. The Allied situation by then was grave. The French armies were recovering from widespread mutiny, the Italians had suffered a major reverse at Caporetto and the Russian Front had collapsed. The Allies were desperate for victory on the Western Front and a lot now rested on the entry of America into the war. This had occurred in April 1917, but all the US could offer was an enormous untrained and inexperienced pool of manpower. It would take time before the American Expeditionary Force (AEF) was combat ready.

Initially Fuller conceived the Cambrai operation as little more than a large-scale tank raid in a sector where the ground had not been turned into an impenetrable bog by shellfire. The St Julien-Poelcappelle attack had showed what the tanks could achieve if they operated on firm ground in close liaison with the infantry. It also showed it was important that the tanks be given tactical objectives that were achievable in light of their operational shortcomings. Speed and mechanical reliability remained a problem.

However, thanks to the Allies' need for a major victory, reinforced by the optimism of General Sir Julian Byng's British 3rd Army, the plan changed into one where the Tanks Corps would breach the German lines, through which the 40,000-strong cavalry corps could pour and on into the enemy rear. It is perhaps one of the great ironies of the evolution of armoured warfare that Cambrai, the most ineptly-conceived of British battles, should contain a daring tactical experiment that would change the very nature of warfare forever.

Cambrai was a key supply point for the German *Siegfried Stellung* (the central part of the Hindenburg Line) and its capture along with Bourlon Ridge would threatened the rear of the German line to the north. However, the German defences at Cambrai were formidable. While the fighting at Ypres ground on interminably, the newly-formed Tank Corps proposed an attack using almost 500 tanks on the much firmer ground to the south and toward the Hindenburg Line. It was agreed that the tanks and infantry, covered by artillery and aircraft, would attack together with the cavalry corps waiting in the wings to exploit any breakthrough.

South-west of Cambrai, the German defences were anchored on the St Quentin Canal and the Canal du Nord, between which lay Marçoing, Havrincourt, Flesquières, Graincourt and Bourlon. This meant that the three corps of General Byng's 3rd Army would be funnelled between the two canals as they fought their way north toward Cambrai. Once through the German front line, they would have to clear Bourlon Wood and get over the St Quentin Canal to get to Cambrai itself. The initial problem facing the Tank Corps was how to break through the Hindenburg Line. This consisted of three lines of mutually supporting trenches protected by great swathes of barbed wire and supported by artillery.

To breach the enemy defences 3rd Army proposed attacking between Bonavis Ridge and the Canal du Nord with two of its five corps, 2nd and 4th, employing 216 tanks to reach the St Quentin Canal at Masnières and Marçoing. To the north 4th Corps, with 108 tanks, was tasked with taking Flesquières Ridge and Bourlon Wood. The enemy had heavily fortified both and on Flesquières Ridge the defenders were well prepared for a tank attack. The cavalry corps would follow up through the breach to secure Cambrai and the crossings of the Sensè River.

In total there were 378 gun tanks, fifty-four supply tanks hauling sledges, thirty-two wire-clearers fitted with grapnels to make gaps for the cavalry, two with bridging equipment and five wireless tanks. For Cambrai the tanks were to be deployed in groups of three, to get over the trenches each was carrying a fascine weighting over a ton. In support of each group of tanks four platoons of infantry were to advance in column, rather than the normal extended line.

Fuller knew that for the Tank Corps surprise was of the essence; any lengthy preliminary bombardment would tip off the Germans and give them time to prepare their defences. Instead, the guns would conduct a rolling barrage as the tanks rolled forward, with aircraft supplementing the guns by bombing forward enemy guns positions and their lines of communication.

All the assault divisions except for the 51st Highlander Division accepted Fuller's operational plan. Their divisional commander, General George Harper, instigated his own tank tactics partly because the ground the 51st had to cover was dotted in a larger number of small fortifications. These inevitably would slow up the advance. Unknown to Harper who was to assault Flesquières, the defending German 54th Division under General Oskar von Watter had made special provision for dealing with tanks. His brother had faced them on the Somme and warned Watter of what to expect. The gunners of Field Artillery Regiment 108 were trained to haul their 77mm field guns from their gun pits so they could engage the tanks with direct rather than indirect afire. This would be much deadlier and ensured a heavy toll was exacted. Watter also ordered his gunners to train using moving targets, guaranteeing the crews kept their aim and their nerve.

The German Army had two types of 77mm field gun in service. The improved Krupp Model 96 was the standard weapon at the outbreak of war, which fired shrapnel. This slightly unusual calibre was chosen because other countries' 75mm guns could be bored out to take German ammunition, but the same could not be done with the 77mm. However, its range soon proved insufficient against contemporary British and French guns. The improved 77mm FK16 was introduced in 1916 to speed up wartime production. Whilst this had a longer range and much higher muzzle velocity it was considerably heavier and therefore not as manoeuvrable. The FK16 fired high-explosive shells.

By the time of Cambrai the Germans recognized that they needed a dedicated light anti-tank gun to protect their infantry. A number of designs were developed but these were only undergoing trials by the summer of 1918. The Rheinmetall 37mm anti-tank gun proved the best and could be manoeuvred by just two men. It only had an effective range of 300m (compared to the 9,100m of the 77mm FK16 field gun), but this would have been adequate against the Allies' slow-moving tanks. If it had been ready earlier then it could have caused the Allies great difficulties especially during the first half of 1918. Luckily for them the war ended before production could begin.

Watter's veteran command had been bloodied in the Battle of Verdun and in the Third Battle of Ypres. It had suffered heavy losses and Allied intelligence rated it as a second-class division. Underestimating the Germans defending Flesquières Ridge would cost the Tank Corps dearly. It would also cause the 51st Highland Division difficulties, which impacted on operations on the flanks.

While there were high hopes a breakthrough could be achieved, there were severe doubts over what would happen afterwards. It was this part of the plan that was fatally flawed. Perhaps a little ironically, the success of the battle rested on the cavalry. Even at this late stage in the war the generals still seemed to imagine that the cavalry could simply gallop through and put the enemy to flight – despite the fact that they would be met by broken terrain as well as enemy machine-guns and artillery.

Crucially the British had no tank or infantry reserves to exploit any rupture of the enemy line. This meant everything rested on the ability of the four cavalry divisions to get through the breach and put the Germans to flight before they could organize a counter-attack. Brigadier John Charteris, Haig's intelligence chief, summed up the situation in his diary, 'We shall be alright at first, afterwards is in the lap of the God of Battle'.

British troops on exercise with a Mark IV female. At Cambrai the infantry advanced in close column rather than the traditional method of extended line. They were followed by trench stop parties whose job was to clear the enemy defences once they had been overrun.

A mixture of Mark IV male and female tanks being transported to the front just before the Battle of Cambrai in November 1917. The sponsons have been retracted into the hulls to reduce their width for shipping.

More tanks moving up for the attack — 378 gun tanks were committed to the assault.

French infantry taking a meal in their muddy dugout. During the second half of 1917 the French army was still recovering from a series of mutinies brought on by the unending bloodletting.

A Belgian machine-gunner on guard in Flanders. He is armed with the French Chauchat M1915 light machine gun. The open-sided magazine allowed in dirt making the weapon prone to jamming. The British Army's lack of progress in Flanders made them look to Cambrai and the Tank Corps.

General Sir Julian Byng, commanding the British 3rd Army, was sure that the tanks could break the German defences at Cambrai. However, his battle plan was far too ambitious and his lack of reserves ultimately doomed the operation.

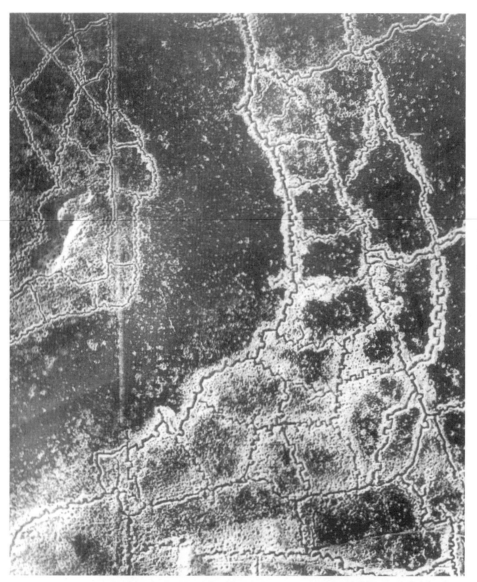

This aerial photo gives some impression of the depth of typical enemy defences the tanks had to overcome. On the right is the German trench line in the Loos-Hulluch area. The myriad of communication trenches created the lattice or patchwork pattern.

German trenches and weapons pits on the Hindenburg Line at Bullecourt.

A very young-looking German soldier with minimal field gear. The Germans first adopted steel helmets in 1916.

Having just unloaded their tanks, British tank crews pose for the camera. Their next task was to extend the sponsons and install the weapons.

Canadian troops examining a German concrete bunker. The Hindenburg Line was dotted with such reinforced strongpoints.

Tanks and infantry advancing at Cambrai in November 1917. This marked the biggest tank battle to date. All eyes were on the Tank Corps.

Chapter Eight

The Allies Strike

At 0600 on 20 November 1917 the Tank Corps attack at Cambrai opened. Their commander Brigadier Sir Hugh Elles rode into battle in a Mark IV male called *Hilda*. The Mark IV was the first British tank to be used en masse and was the main type that fought at Cambrai. Apart from problems experienced by the 51st Highland Division everything went pretty much to plan. Heralded by their roaring engines and great billowing clouds of petrol fumes the massed ranks of 470 tanks crawled into No Man's Land and through the chaos caused by the opening bombardment.

Along with the gun tanks and their supporting infantry came something equally new in the realms of armoured warfare, wire-pulling tanks, radio tanks and supply tanks ready to assist wherever they were needed. Despite the commitment of this huge tank force, the British Mark IVs were eventually to succumb to the Germans' determined defence and heavy firepower.

A tank thwarted attempts by the 20th (Light) Division to cross the St Quentin Canal at Masnières after it fell through the bridge. At Flesquières the 51st Highlanders became separated from their tanks. Upon crossing Flesquières Ridge the exposed tanks, whose supporting infantry were lagging behind, were met by well-trained and determined German gunners. This hold up left the divisions on the flanks exposed to enemy fire. The delay was attributed to the German Field Artillery Regiment 108 and General Harper's reluctance to commit his reserves. The 51st Highlanders lost twenty-eight of their tanks, though not all of these were to German artillery. One of the effects the German fire had was to cause the tanks to lurch and veer all over the place. The result was that many became bogged down and had to be abandoned by their crews.

The 6th Division captured Ribécourt and Marçoing in the centre but the cavalry were late and subsequently repulsed at Noyelles. West of Flesquières, the 62nd (2nd West Riding) Division forced their way through to Havrincourt and almost to the woods on Bourlon Ridge; while the 36th (Ulster) Division on the British left reached the Bapaume-Cambrai Road.

The attrition rate for the Tank Corps was severe. By the end of 20 November

179 tanks were reported out of action, with sixty-five destroyed, seventy-one broken down and forty-three ditched. This sacrifice had not been in vain, however. A breach 4,000 yards deep and six miles wide had been cut into the Germans defences at the cost of less than 4,000 casualties. In England the church bells rang out at the news of the victory. If the advance had been stopped at this stage and kept within Fuller's original concept of a limited tank raid then it would have been a remarkable victory.

Supported by 100 tanks and 430 guns the British attacked the woods on Bourlon Ridge on 23 November but made little progress. Four days later the 62nd Division, aided by thirty tanks, renewed the attack. Once in control of the crest of the ridge the British dug in to endure a deluge of 16,000 German shells. At 0700 on 30 November 1917 the Germans launched a counter-offensive at Cambrai with the intention of retaking the Bourlon salient as well as attacking around Havrincourt. By the end of the Battle of Cambrai the British had suffered 44,000 causalities for very little territorial gain. Nonetheless British tank tactics had proved largely sound and shaken the Germans.

A German officer from General Headquarters briefing members of the Reichstag on the British use of tanks at Cambrai reported: 'The enemy employed them in unexpectedly large numbers. Where, after a very thoroughgoing blanketing of our positions with smoke clouds, they made surprise assaults, the nerves of our fellows frequently could not stand the strain. In such cases, they broke through our forward lines, cleared the way for their infantry, appeared at our rear, produced local panics and broke up in confusion the arrangements for directing the battle.'

Despite armoured warfare still being in its infancy the generals demanded the initial breakthrough be followed up. Because the cavalry failed to exploit the situation it fell to the infantry and the remaining tanks to widen the breach. Perhaps predictably the Germans managed to block any further advances and the remaining British reserves were expended gaining ground measured in just yards. Frustratingly in places the British were even forced back beyond their original start line. However, the Tank Corps could not held responsible for these subsequent disasters. At Gouzeaucourt it gained fresh credit when a timely tank counter-attack halted the German advance. This proved that tanks could capture and hold ground when the need arose.

While Cambrai showed what the tank could achieve with the element of surprise, operating en masse and with adequate infantry and artillery support, the failure to exploit the initial breakthrough remained a vexed issue. Rather unfairly, Elles and Fuller were criticized for not holding back part of the Tank Corps as a reserve. This seemed to miss the point that a smaller attacking force would have achieved a smaller breakthrough, which any reserves would have struggled to capitalize on.

What the battle also clearly demonstrated was that while the Mark IV was a vast improvement on its predecessors, it was simply too slow and heavy to exploit any breakthrough. The cavalry were no longer up to such a task, so what was needed was a lighter and faster tank that could charge through a breach and into the enemy's rear area. The French had already come to this conclusion with the development of the FT-17.

In London leading politicians were far from happy about the outcome of the Battle of Cambrai. 'This action was grossly bungled', said Prime Minister Lloyd George, 'and the tank success was thrown away through the ineptitude of the High Command'. In his memoirs Lloyd George was more specific, pointing the finger firmly at General Byng:

> The first onset of the Tanks, on 20th November, was a brilliant success. Within a few hours the Hindenburg line was broken by these inexorable machines, and a penetration effected in the enemy lines as deep as that which had been achieved after months of terrible fighting and colossal losses on the Somme and at Passchendaele. It is generally acknowledged now that the advance was badly muddled by General Byng and that he could, even with the resources at his command, have made a better job of it. But what converted victory into defeat was a total lack of reserves.

This was grossly unfair. General Byng had little choice but renew his attack at Cambrai with just 130 tanks. The Tank Corps were not given enough time to recover the 114 tanks that had broken down or become stuck. These might have made a difference. Lloyd George was right about the lack of reserves and Haig was well aware of this. Elles and Fuller had set their sights on achievable goals for the Tank Corps, Haig and Byng had not and it was they who had not met Lloyd George's expectations.

It was not an altogether auspicious start to massed mechanized warfare. The Germans, however, finally began to take note of the possibilities offered by the tank. Ironically, while the Mark IV became the most numerically significant tank of the war, it also became the most numerous German tank. The Germans gathered up all the Mark IVs they captured at Cambrai and the earlier actions at Charleroi and refurbished them. In German service the Mark IV was dubbed the *Beute Panzerwagen IV* or 'captured armoured vehicle 4'. In December 1917 the German Army formed four tank companies employing around forty captured Mark IVs. However, the first tank-to-tank battle did not occur until April 1918, when cumbersome German-built A7Vs took on British Mark IVs at the Second Battle of Villers-Bretonneux. This heralded the true birth of tank warfare.

Jubilant British troops hitch a ride – the morale of the British 3rd Army was understandably high in light of the massed tank fleet spearheading the attack at Cambrai on 20 November 1917.

Mark IV male with unditching beam deployed for crossing enemy trenches. In total 432 Mark IVs were committed at Cambrai.

A British Mark I gun carrier bearing a 60-pounder gun. The weapon's wheels have been removed and chained to the sides. This carrier's potential as offensive mobile artillery was never realised. Just fifty were built and they ended up being used as supply and recovery tanks.

A Wire Cutter (hence WC) Mark IV broken down at Cambrai being used as an observation post.

To counter British tanks the Germans used flamethrowers and artillery. Flamethrowers were used by stormtroopers as part of their assault weaponry. The Germans deployed two man-portable variants, the *Kleinflammenwerfer* (small flamethrower) known as the 'Kleif' and the *Wechselapparat* or 'Wex'. A larger trench-based variant was also used known as the *Grossflammenwerfer*.

The shattered remains of a female tank – in total the Germans destroyed sixty-five tanks during the Tank Corps assault at Cambrai.

Medics collect casualties amidst a tank graveyard. At Flesquières German field guns were manhandled forward to fire directly at the exposed tanks as they came over the ridge.

A disabled Mark IV tank near Cambrai. Both tracks have come off.

German soldiers recovering a captured Mark IV. A total of seventy-one tanks broke down and another forty-three became stuck at Cambrai.

This female tank picked a fight with a tree in November 1917 and lost.

Remains of a female tank captured at Cambrai. The Tank Corps lost 179 tanks on 20 November 1917.

A re-badged female tank at Armentières. At the end of 1917 the German Army formed four tank companies using forty captured British Mark IVs.

German infantry supporting a captured British tank. The German High Command was slow to accept the tank and development of the German A7V *Sturmpanzerwagen* was slow.

German troops familiarize themselves with an enemy tank now under new ownership.

Chapter Nine

Tank versus Tank: Villers-Bretonneux

T hanks to the British naval blockade the German population was suffering by 1918. German submarines had failed to starve Britain into submission or stop the shipping of American forces to the Western Front. Gathering his last reserves, Ludendorff gambled on a knockout blow against the British who he considered the most vulnerable. If this could be achieved the Allies might sue for peace and bring an end to the conflict.

Even by this stage of the war the German High Command was not receptive to the tank. From their perspective those deployed by the British and French had not achieved truly decisive results. They decided what was needed was better infantry tactics that would allow for greater initiative and individual firepower.

The Germans felt that the anti-tank rifle, submachine gun and light machine gun offered much better prospects for achieving a breakthrough. In 1918 they produced the first purpose-built anti-tank rifle called the Mauser T-Gewehr. It fired a 13mm round and was based on big-game hunters' elephant guns. This was issued to specially-formed anti-tank detachments whose job was to hunt down tanks.

Nonetheless, a rudimentary tank programme was instigated. The first German tank, the unwieldy A7V *Sturmpanzerwagen*, went into production in October 1917. Although 100 were ordered only twenty had armoured bodies as the rest were used as cargo-carriers. With a crew of seventeen, the A7V was a lumbering armoured box armed with a 57mm Maxim-Nordenfelt gun mounted at the front and six 7.92mm machine guns. It bore a greater resemblance to the French box-type heavy tanks than to the British rhomboid design. This was surprising as the Germans operated British tanks. Weighing some 33 tons when combat-loaded, the A7V could manage a top cross-country speed of 4mph and a range of about 20 miles.

The *Sturmpanzerwagen* was little more than an armoured gun platform for infantry support. As a result the design suffered from all the same problems that plagued the French St-Chamond and Schneider tanks. Its shape and size meant it was very poorly balanced and as the engine was underpowered it had very poor cross-country capability. A female variant was designed with two machine guns replacing the main armament, but only one of these saw combat before being converted to take the 57mm gun. As the Germans only had a handful of A7Vs they were not really a factor in their Spring 1918 offensive. Instead they relied on their new infantry tactics to carry them through.

Peace with Bolshevik Russia permitted Ludendorff to redeploy fifty divisions from the Eastern Front. Crucially these included troops trained in the latest infiltration tactics. They employed a new type of soldier dubbed the 'stormtrooper', some armed with the new Bergmann MP18 submachine gun. The stormtroopers moved swiftly through enemy lines leaving strongpoints to be mopped up by subsequent waves of infantry. General Oskar von Hutier devised these new tactics (from which the Nazi concept of Blitzkrieg or lightning war was to evolve) and they were first used on the Eastern Front at Riga in 1917.

By March Ludendorff had massed sixty-three divisions facing the 56-mile long sector between Arras and St Quentin held by the British 5th and 3rd Armies. These mustered just twenty-six divisions – Gough's 5th Army was spread especially thinly in the south where it had been deployed to recuperate after its mauling at Passchendaele. Although better organized, Byng's 3rd Army, which lay to the north, would be exposed if 5th Army gave ground.

On 21 March 1918 some 9,000 artillery pieces and mortars heralded the German Michael offensive. This was the opening stage of a whole series of attacks designed to crack open the Western Front. General von Hutier's 18th Army set about the Gough's 5th Army while General Georg von de Marwitz attacked Byng's 3rd Army. The A7V proved mechanically unreliable and when five went into action on the 21st north of the St Quentin Canal three broke down.

Despite advancing up to 40 miles in places, within a week the Germans began to lose momentum. By 28 March Hutier had come to a temporary halt and by 5 April Marwitz had been stopped by British and Australian troops at Villers-Bretonneux some 10 miles short of his objective, Amiens. In two weeks of fighting Ludendorff suffered 250,000 casualties, which included a large number of his elite stormtroopers. Nonetheless, keeping the pressure up, on 9 April Ludendorff launched Operation Georgette to the north against Flanders with the aim of threatening the Channel ports.

The Allies reeled back in two areas under the shock of the German offensives. Ludendorff gained some ground south of Dunkirk and north of Arras. South of Arras, though, he achieved an even greater penetration extending to Reims. Allied tanks deployed in the defence were used as mobile pillboxes, which posed little problem for the highly-mobile stormtroopers. However, when the tanks were combined they greatly helped in stemming the German tide.

If Ludendorff succeeded in taking Villers-Bretonneux plus the high ground between there and Cachy then German artillery would be able to dominate Amiens. The French alert to the danger moved forces including the French Foreign Legion to Bois de Blangy about four miles west of Villers-Bretonneux along with A Company, 1st Tank Battalion of the British Tank Corps. The tanks were deployed to conduct 'Savage Rabbit' tactics whereby they lay in ambush positions ready to surprise infiltrating enemy troops. A Company was equipped with patched-up Mark IVs. No. 1 Section was commanded by Captain J. C. Brown, MC with three tanks – two female and one male. The single male was commanded by 2nd Lieutenant Frank Mitchell. Apart from its short 6-pounder guns and no steering tail it was little different in appearance to the original Mark I.

A second British tank type was involved in the coming battle – consisting of seven British Medium A Whippets from C Battalion, Tank Corps under Captain T. R. Price. At 14 tons, the Whippet required a crew of three, was armed only with four machine guns and could manage 8mph. This was Britain's answer to the FT-17, although it was twice the weight of the French tank and required an extra crewman.

Captain Brown's tanks were given a warm reception when they moved into the woods just to the north of Cachy. On the night of 23 April a German spotter plane flew over the Bois l'Abbe and dropped flares. These were followed by high-explosive rounds and mustard gas shells, which forced No.1 Section to withdraw to the western edge of the woods.

By this stage the Germans were short of troops and ammunition, which precluded anything more than a spoiling attack in the Villers-Bretonneux and Cachy area. However, they had fourteen A7V *Sturmpanzerwagen* available for the operation. These were divided into three groups, with the first comprising three tanks heading for Villers-Bretonneux, the second made up of seven tanks on the right flank heading for Bois d'Aquenne, and the third with four tanks driving on Cachy.

In the meantime two of Lieutenant Mitchell's crew were overcome by gas and had to be evacuated. Nearby wounded infantrymen informed Brown and Mitchell that enemy troops were in Villers-Bretonneux. It was decided that they would counter-attack under the covering fire of a battery of 18-pounder guns in the area.

At 0845 on 24 April 1918 Brown set off in Mitchell's tank, which deployed nearest the woods with the two female tanks on the right. 'As the wood was still thick with gas we wore our masks', recalled Mitchell, 'while cranking up a third member of my crew collapsed and I had to leave him behind propped up against a tree trunk'. A crewman from one of the females was sent over to help, but Mitchell was still two crew short.

At 0930, when they reached the defences of the Cachy Switch Line, an infantryman warned them of the presence of German tanks. Mitchell saw three objects heading toward eastern Cachy followed by enemy infantry. The fourth German tank with the group, called *Elfriede*, had got lost in the fog, veered north and fallen into a quarry. Captain Brown ran to warn the females while Mitchell swung right to move parallel to the nearest German tank under 2nd Lieutenant Wilhelm Biltz called *Nixe*.

Mitchell's left-hand 6-pounder began to fire on *Nixe* but there was no response, while his forward Lewis gun opened up on the German infantry. He then turned his tank to face the Germans. Mitchell later wrote: 'Suddenly there was a noise like a storm of hail beating against our right wall and the tank became alive with splinters. It was a broadside of armour-piercing bullets. . . . The crew lay flat on the floor. I ordered the driver to go straight ahead and we gradually drew clear, but not before our faces were splintered. Steel helmets protected our heads.'

Lieutenant Biltz had put his tank into reverse and opened up with everything he had. Mitchell, hoping to get a clear shot, halted but this convinced Biltz the British tank was knocked out so he turned on the two females. He hit both, ripping holes in their armour and forcing them to withdraw.

In the meantime Mitchell rumbled forward, recalling that at 1020, 'The gunner ranged steadily nearer and then I saw a shell burst high up on the forward part of the German tank. It was a direct hit. He obtained a second hit almost immediately lower down on the side facing us and then a third in the same region. It was splendid shooting for a man whose eyes were swollen by gas and who was working his gun single-handed, owing to the shortage of crew.'

Biltz's crew were in a bad way. Mitchell's first hit had killed the front gunner, mortally wounded two others and injured a further three. Afraid that a box of hand grenades might explode, the crew bailed out. However, Mitchell's other two hits did little damage and *Nixe*'s engines continued running. Biltz and his crew returned to their tank and drove 1.25 miles before the engines seized up through lack of oil.

Mitchell engaged the other two A7Vs and when they withdrew southwards he assumed he had seen them off. He then continued to patrol the Switch Line and shelled the German infantry. It was at 1100 that the Whippets entered the fray, driving from northern Cachy and into the midst of the enemy infantry. Firing their machine-guns, they scattered the Germans left and right.

Captain Price had been informed incorrectly, as it transpired, that he was attacking unsupported enemy soldiers. Instead he ran into the other two A7Vs, *Schnuck* commanded by 2nd Lieutenant Albert Mueller and *Siegfried* under 2nd Lieutenant Friedrich-Wilhelm Bitter. The latter moved forward and opened fire along with supporting artillery. Price's tanks had no way of defending themselves against the A7Vs' 57mm guns. Suddenly one of the Whippets lurched to a halt with smoke pouring from it and a second burst into flames. It is unclear who hit them, but this unexpected resistance had the desired effect. The rest of the Whippets then began to withdraw on Cachy but only three made it undamaged after two of them broke down.

Lieutenant Mitchell's luck also ran out. He had already been accidentally bombed by a friendly aircraft that thought his tank was German. This error is perhaps easy to understand in light of the Germans redeploying captured Mark IVs. Spotting a German tank at a range of some 1,000 yards Mitchell opened fire, but this drew the attention of a German mortar crew. 'We had been hit at last', recalled Mitchell, 'We got out and made for the nearest trench some 50 yards back. It was about 12.45pm.'

For his bravery during the engagement between Cachy and Villers-Bretonneux, Mitchell was awarded the Military Cross, while his right-hand gunner Sergeant J. R. Mckenzie received the Military Medal. Mitchell's citation read:

> For most conspicuous gallantry and devotion to duty in action against enemy tanks at Cachy on April 24, 1918. This officer was in command of a male tank in action east of the Cachy Switch Line, when hostile tanks came in action. He fought his tank with great gallantry and manoeuvred it with much skill in order to bring the most effective fire on the enemy one, but to avoid offering a greater target than possible. As a result of his skilful handling of his tank and his control of fire, he was able to register five direct hits on the enemy tank and put it out of action. Throughout he showed the greatest coolness and initiative.

Villers-Bretonneux showed the Mark IV and Whippet to be far more manoeuvrable than the unwieldy *Sturmpanzerwagen*. However, the females and the Whippets armed with just machine guns were unable to fight them on anything like equal terms. This meant only Mitchell's male Mark IV was able to take on the three AV7s. The world had witnessed its very first tank versus tank battle.

A captured British Mark IV female rearmed with German Maxim machine guns. The redeployment of British tanks by the German Army meant Allied aircraft sometimes mistakenly attacked their own tanks.

The Medium Mark A Whippet tank came into service in 1918. It was designed by William Tritton and built by Fosters of Lincoln. Although only armed with machine guns it was capable of twice the speed of the Mark IV.

The German High Command was very slow to adopt the tank placing their faith instead in the stormtrooper for victory. This young stormtrooper is armed with the Bergmann MP18 submachine gun introduced in 1918. The round object is the 32-round 'snail' magazine used on the Luger semi-automatic pistol, which was adapted for the MP18.

The German A7V *Sturmpanzerwagen* went into production in October 1917, but only twenty of these cumbersome land fortresses were built.

The *Sturmpanzerwagen* was more akin to the French St-Chamond and Schneider tanks than British designs. It required a crew of seventeen.

The A7V/U was being developed as a copy of the British rhomboid shape but did not go into production before the Armistice.

An AV7 tank at Roye 30 miles south-east of Amiens on 21 March 1918. The crew preferred to ride on the outside of the hull when not in combat.

Two AV7s ready for action – this cumbersome tank was armed with a nose-mounted 57mm Maxim-Nordenfelt gun and six 7.92mm MG08 machine guns. *Hagen* was lost at Fremicourt during the summer of 1918.

In this graphic dramatisation, AV7s bear down on Villers-Bretonneux.

An artist's impression of Lieutenant Frank Mitchell's Mark IV male engaging an AV7 at Villers-Bretonneux.

At Villers-Bretonneux the Whippet could not cope with the AV7's heavy gun. Two were knocked out and two broke down.

An AV7 named *Schnuck* was captured by the New Zealand Division on 31 August 1918 at Fremicourt. Its new owners have marked it 'KEEP CLEAR' and 'NZ Division'.

The Germans were also slow to appreciate the benefits of other types of armoured vehicle. Just twenty Ehrhardt armoured cars were built and these were sent to the Eastern Front.

Developed in 1915, the Büssing A5P armoured car was massive and unwieldy. The German Army preferred the Ehrhardt design so just three A5Ps were ever built and these again were sent to the Eastern Front.

Chapter Ten

Renaults at Soissons

During the first half of 1918 the Allied commanders husbanded their reserves ready for when the German offensive lost momentum and they could counter-attack. By July 1918 it was evident that the Germans had been held. The three Allied commanders, Foch (who was CinC of all Allied forces), Haig and General John J. Pershing of the AEF planned three offensives. The French would strike along the Aisne and Marne rivers, the British at Amiens and the Americans in the St Mihiel salient south of Verdun.

The French Army began to take delivery of its new Renault light tank in early 1918. By February that year over 4,000 had been ordered comprising 1,000 machine-gun tanks, 1,830 37mm-gun tanks, 970 75mm-gun tanks and 200 unarmed signal tanks. Although the first four FT-17s had appeared in September 1917 they had not been handed over to the army until the following March. The first units to be equipped with them were three battalions of the 501st *Régiment de Chars de Combat.*

The FT-17 first saw action on 31 May 1918 at Retz Forest during the German offensive. Although the French light tanks were only committed in small groups, they performed well in supporting the infantry and helped check the German advance. To support the Renaults in the field a maintenance workshop was set up at Bourrin in May 1918. This soon gained a reputation for the speed and efficiency with which it got the tanks back to the front.

In June 1918 British GHQ ordered the horns and cupolas on all British tanks be painted with prominent red and white stripes to distinguish them from captured vehicles being used by the German Army. The following month the most decisive use of tanks to date involving Australian, British and American troops was achieved thanks to precise tank and infantry co-ordination. This was due to Lieutenant General John Monash, commander of the Australian Corps. Monash was considered an outstanding commander and had led an Australian division at Passchendaele. He planned the reduction of the Hamel salient as a tank-led operation which he put before General Rawlinson on 21 June. This required two tank battalions that would capture the ground for the infantry to mop up. The operation was to be supported by a creeping barrage, counter-battery fire and smoke – but no preliminary bombardment. In the air support would include fighters and bombers. Hamel was to prove a model for future combined operations.

Following Bullecourt in 1917, when they had been left exposed, Australian troops were not terribly keen on tanks. Monash therefore made special efforts to familiarize his men with the Tank Corps' brand-new Mark V. At Vaux-en-Amienois, a village north-west of Amiens, the Tank Corps trained with the Australians to acquaint them with current tank tactics. It was vital that trust and confidence was restored. Monash recalled:

> Red flags marked enemy machine gun posts; real wire entanglements were laid out to show how easily the Tanks could mow them down; real trenches were dug for the Tanks to leap and straddle and search with fire; real rifle grenades were fired by the infantry to indicate to the tanks the enemy strong points which were molesting or impeding their advance. The Tanks would throw themselves upon these places, and pirouetting round and round, would blot them out, much as a man's heel would crush a scorpion.

It seems Monash's men were suitably impressed. To improve liaison and esprit de corps the Australians named the tanks they would be working alongside. Furthermore Monash, with Brigadier-General Courage, commander of the 5th Tank Brigade, as well as developing new tactics also ensured that there was no confusion in the chain of command. He recorded:

> Firstly, each Tank was, for tactical purposes, to be treated as an Infantry weapon; from the moment it entered the battle until the objectives had been gained it was to be under the exclusive orders of the Infantry Commander to whom it has been assigned.
>
> Secondly, the deployed line of tanks was to advance, level with the Infantry, and pressing close up to the barrage. This of course, subjected the Tanks, which towered high above the heads of the neighbouring infantry, to the danger of being struck by any of our own shells which happened to fall a little short. Tank experts, consulted beforehand, considered therefore that it was not practicable for the Tanks to follow close behind an artillery barrage. The Battle of Hamel proved that it was.

On 4 July Monash launched his operation led by the Australian 4th Division with sixty Mark V tanks. To mask the approach of the tanks they were assembled under the noise of aircraft buzzing overhead. They then advanced through the mist at 0310 hours with the infantry close up to the creeping barrage. It was all over in ninety-three minutes. At the cost of 775 Australian and 134 American casualties they captured almost 1,500 prisoners, two field guns, 171 machine guns and twenty-six trench mortars.

The last of Ludendorff's major Spring Offensive operations opened on 15 July, heralding the Second Battle of the Marne. Ludendorff wanted to attack the British in Flanders but in order to draw Allied forces away from Belgium launched a diversionary attack against the French along the Marne. He hoped to divide the French forces and surround the city of Reims. The German 1st and 3rd Armies were launched against the French 4th Army east of Reims, while the German 7th Army attacked the French 6th Army to the west. The attack to the east went badly and was stopped on the first day. To the west the Germans got over the Marne, but some Allied units, including the US 3rd Division, held long enough for reinforcements to arrive and stabilize the situation. The French army then counter-attacked.

For the Second Battle of the Marne the French deployed their massed tanks using the Cambrai method without any artillery preparation. In June the French assembled their reserves at Beauvais and Epernay with a view to striking the flank of any fresh German advances. The first group, under General Mangin, had been used to counter a German attack on 9 June, and was redeployed further east to a position on the western flank of the German salient between Soissons and Reims that bulged towards the Marne. The French plan was that while the 9th and 5th Armies held down German attacks at the base of the salient and on the eastern flank, the 10th and 6th Armies would counter-attack eastwards trapping the Germans between the Aisne and the Marne.

At 0435 on 18 July Mangin's 10th Army (which included two British and two American divisions) struck using some 400 tanks, the bulk of which were Renaults. On Mangin's inner flank the left of Degoutte's 6th Army (including seven American divisions) joined in an hour and a half later after the customary preliminary bombardment. To ease pressure on the centre of the salient and on the right the line was strengthened by British and American reinforcements. On the first day, thanks to the sudden appearance of massed French tanks Mangin's troops advanced four miles and a little further on the second. He was then brought to a standstill while the Germans withdrew to the Vesle though they left behind 25,000 prisoners.

Lloyd George continued to champion the use of tanks by the British and French armies, '. . . the tactics of the massed tank attack, which proved so successful in breaking the German line at Cambrai… were adopted by the Allies repeatedly … As we have seen they were the spearpoint of the French thrust on July 18th which was the turn of the tide. Their nimble little tanks dashed though the German lines and created confusion and dismay.'

Following the Michael offensive in March and the May Artois offensive, the Germans had achieved remarkable success. However, the arrival of half a million American 'doughboys' had tilted the strategic balance. By late July the Americans had helped the French defeat the last German offensive. Allied supreme commander General Foch now wanted to maintain the pressure with a series of offensives. These were to open at Amiens led by Monash's Australian Corps and the Canadian Corps under General Arthur Currie, spearheaded by a massive tank force. They were to be supported by the French to the south. The British Army was then to conduct a series of offensives further north though August and September.

Hindenburg, the Kaiser and Ludendorff in conference. By July 1918 it was evident that their Spring Offensive had been brought to a halt, which meant inevitable Allied counter-attacks.

The British Mark V, successor to the Mark IV, had a raised cupola at the rear for improved visibility and needed only one driver. It went into production at the end of 1917 and saw action the following year.

The Australian commander General Monash was a keen enthusiast of the tank concept and conceived the Hamel attack as a tank-led all-arms operation.

In June 1918 Monash's Australian troops trained with the Tank Corps and watched the tanks 'pirouetting round and round' on dummy enemy positions in order to 'blot them out'.

The Mark V first saw combat on 4 July 1918 at the Battle of Hamel supporting Monash's Australian Corps. This limited operation proved to be a great success.

At the Second Battle of the Marne the French infantry were supported by 400 tanks. These men belong to General Gouraud's 4th Army that held the Germans east of Reims.

Tank crew examining the German anti-tank rifle, which came into service in 1918. The Germans also developed a 37mm anti-tank gun but it was not ready for production before the war ended.

The bulk of the French tanks deployed at Soissons comprised Renault FT-17s armed with machine guns or 37mm guns. British Prime Minister David Lloyd George described them as 'nimble little tanks' that 'created confusion' behind enemy lines.

The two-man FT-17 was extremely cramped but far more capable than the St-Chamond and Schneider tanks.

French troops examine a German AV7 tank. It seems to have become a magnet for graffiti artists.

Chapter Eleven

Amiens Sledgehammer

General Rawlinson's offensive at Amiens in the summer of 1918 was based on a bold gamble. This was at a crucial moment in the war when it had been finally accepted by the moribund infantry commanders that the tank represented the key to eventual victory. The Allies were encouraged by the French counter-attack on the Marne when using a swarm of tanks they had achieved startling success. This had come at a cost amounting to 184 heavy tanks, some 57 per cent of the total. Nonetheless, it was decided to commit every single British tank brigade to the attack at Amiens, except for the 1st that at the time was converting from the Mark IV to the new Mark V tank. If anything went wrong or losses were too heavy at Amiens, it could result in the British Army losing its tank fleet in one go.

The Allies' sledgehammer force at Amiens was provided by three whole tank brigades from the British Tank Corps totalling eleven tank battalions. It comprised the largest concentration of tanks ever assembled during the First World War – numbering 324 heavy tanks and ninety-six medium tanks in the British sector with seventy-two light tanks in the French. Supporting them were an additional 120 supply tanks and twenty-two gun-carrier tanks, giving a total of 634 tanks committed to the battle. It was notable because of their heavy losses on the Marne that the French infantry had to go over the top largely without tank support.

Two other 'armoured' units were to be involved. Firstly the 17th Armoured Car Battalion, equipped with sixteen vehicles, had only come into existence in April 1918. This Tank Corps formation was issued with Austin armoured cars which had originally been built for export to Russia. The Russian Army had ordered three batches of Austins before the Revolution finally but an end to any further deliveries. Featuring double turrets they were armed with the Hotchkiss M1914 machine gun rather than Vickers or Maxim guns in British service. It was a unique unit within the Tank Corps as the RNAS had handed its armoured cars over the Army's Machine Gun Corps in the summer of 1915 to form the Light Armoured Motor Batteries. Secondly there were two Canadian Motor Machine Gun Brigades. They operated lightly armoured, open-topped trucks designed to move machine guns, mortars and infantry about. Essentially these operated as weapons carriers and lightly-armoured personnel carriers rather than true armoured fighting vehicles.

At Amiens Rawlinson, now an enthusiast of the tank, followed the example set by Monash and deployed the largest practicable force of armour and the smallest practicable force of infantry – some eight assault divisions. North to south in Rawlinson's 4th Army's sector lay the British 3rd Corps, the Australian Corps and the Canadian Corps. The 10th Tank Battalion was assigned to 3rd Corps while the 5th and 4th Tank Brigades (each with four tank battalions) were with the Australians and Canadian respectively. The Australian Corps was also supported by the 17th Armoured Car Battalion. The 3rd Tank Brigade, with two battalions of Whippets, acted in support of the cavalry units. South of the Canadians was General Debeney's French 1st Army with three corps facing Moreuil.

The attack opened on 8 August 1918. At 0420 Monash recalled: 'A great illumination lights up the Eastern horizon: and instantly the whole complex organization, extending far back to areas almost beyond earshot of the guns, begins to move forward: everyman, every unit, every vehicle and every tank on the appointed tasks and to their designated goals, sweeping on relentlessly and irresistibly.' The exhausted Germans were taken completely by surprise. Rawlinson's 4th Army advanced over seven miles in less than nine hours. By early afternoon 4th Army and the French 1st Army had taken their initial objectives of Warfusée and Moreuil, followed by Bayonvillers, Guilleaucourt and Hangest.

Regarding the Battle of Amiens Lloyd George recorded in his memoirs: 'Four hundred and fifteen fighting tanks went over the top at zero hour that morning, and in all the engagements of the succeeding days, tanks played their part smashing a way for the infantry, crashing through entanglements, sweeping across trenches, everywhere scattering and stampeding the enemy forces, circumventing machine gun nests and receiving as little hurt from their sting as from ant-heaps in the path of a rhinoceros.'

Having learned the lesson of Cambrai, a mixed force of armour cars, cavalry and Whippets was assembled as the follow-up force to immediately exploit the breakthrough. Co-operation between the cavalry and tanks was poor, but towed across No Man's Land by the tanks the armoured cars were unleashed in the German rear. In the Morcourt valley the armoured cars and the tanks turned the Germans' defences, despite an anti-aircraft gun acting in an anti-tank role.

That first day the Tank Corps losses were very heavy. By 9 August just 145 tanks were available, the following day sixty-three and by the 11th the number was down to thirty-eight. By this stage the battle had lost its momentum. The lurching British Mark IV did not make for a stable gun platform, nor did its restricted vision and poor field of fire help. In reality few German soldiers were actually killed by British tank fire. None of this mattered, however, as the tank had helped smash German morale once and for all. Ludendorff and his generals were shaken by this dramatic turn of events.

Unfortunately the tanks were simply not fast or mechanically reliable enough to keep up with the retreating Germans. Likewise the cavalry could do little in the face of German machine-gun and artillery fire. Nonetheless, new innovations in armoured warfare were tried. For example night attacks were conducted in co-ordination with aircraft. Also a number of tank-versus-tank encounters took place continued right until the end of the war.

Although Ludendorff was able to stabilize the front and hold any further Allied advances the damage was done. German morale was irretrievably broken. Ludendorff belatedly recognized that the tank was a game-changer. On 30 September 1918 he reported, 'It is not, however, the low strengths of our divisions which make our position serious but rather the tanks which appear by surprise in ever increasing numbers.... Owing to the effect of the tanks our operations on the Western Front have now practically assumed the character of a game of chance.'

Not all Germans were prepared to accept that the tank was the reason for their defeat. If anything, Amiens showed just how vulnerable the tank was to direct artillery fire. General von der Marwitz argued: 'Tanks are no bogey for the front line troops who have artillery in close support. For instance, a battery-sergeant-major with his own gun destroyed 4 tanks; one battery destroyed 14; and a single division in one day 40. In another instance, a smart corporal climbed onto a tank and put the crew out of action with his revolver, firing through the aperture. A lance corporal was successful in putting a tank out of action with a hand grenade.' Despite such bravery the Germans acknowledged Amiens as a British victory and called 8 August the 'Black Day'.

Throughout the summer Foch launched a major offensive along the entire front with tanks once again playing their part. In the early autumn, in a series of well-executed offensives led by tanks, the American Army cleared the Argonne to the south-east of Reims and the British broke out beyond Le Cateau, although the Germans were able to fall back in an orderly manner. Nonetheless, time was running out for the German military as they sought to avoid the inevitable.

A column of Mark V tanks moving up to the front. The Battle of Amiens saw the largest concentration of tanks ever assembled during the First World War.

Armoured trucks of the Canadian Motor Machine Gun Brigades. One of the crew is wearing a captured German helmet. Serving with the Canadian Independent Force, these units provided mobile fire support and acted as armoured personnel carriers.

At Amiens the Tank Corps also fielded the 17th Armoured Car Battalion equipped with Austin armoured cars originally intended for the Russian Army.

A Canadian adorns a supporting tank with a maple leaf ready for the attack.

A British 18-pounder field gun deploying to support the tanks. The bulk of the tanks were assigned to the Australian and Canadian Corps. Only a single battalion served with the British 3rd Corps.

German prisoners pass a Mark V tank on the Amiens-Roye Road on 8 August 1918.

Canadians conferring with a tank crew whose tank has thrown a track. A passing French artillery crew look on with interest.

Canadian troops and their tanks passing German prisoners on 9 August 1918.

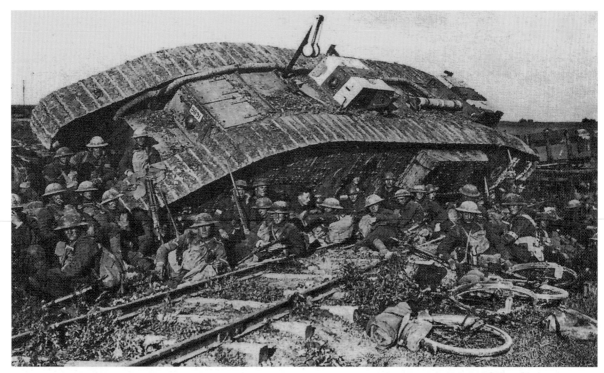

Troops taking a break by a Mark V tank that slipped off a railway embankment. Infantry were first carried into battle in tanks at Amiens in 1918. The Mark V* provided extra interior space but was not terribly successful.

The crew of this Canadian armoured truck were caught by enemy fire. It appears, judging from the empty ammo belts and empty ammo boxes, that they ran out of ammunition.

New Zealanders with a captured German Mauser M1918 anti-tank rifle.

Canadian troops resting by an unarmed Renault signal tank on the Arras-Cambrai road on 1 September 1918.

Observation tanks on a flooded road.

Chapter Twelve

St Mihiel Debut

To the north tanks were deployed to support the Canadian assault on the Drocourt-Quéant Line near Arras. For the Canadian Expeditionary Force 2 September 1918 was a momentous day as its members received seven Victoria Crosses for individual acts of bravery during the attack. Two of these were for liaising with the tanks whilst under heavy fire.

Lieutenant Colonel Peck's men of the 16th (Canadian Scottish) Battalion, after capturing their first objective at Cagnicourt, were held up by heavy machine-gun fire. Peck, also under sniper, fire pushed forward to spot the enemy's positions, and then exposed himself again to find the supporting tanks and give them firing directions. Peck's VC citation noted, 'He then went out under the most intense artillery and machine gun fire, intercepted the tanks, gave them necessary directions . . . His magnificent display of courage and fine qualities of leadership enabled the advance to be continued, although always under heavy artillery and machine-gun fire, and contributed largely to the success of the brigade attack.'

When the right flank of his battalion was held up, Lance-Corporal Will Metcalf, also with the 16th Battalion, likewise dashed through enemy fire to a passing tank and directed it to the enemy strongpoint. He was later wounded. As Metcalf was born in America he is also one of only six Americans to win the VC. His citation recorded:

For most conspicuous bravery, initiative and devotion to duty in attack, when, the right flank of the battalion being held up, he realised the situation and rushed forward under intense machine-gun fire to a passing Tank on the left. With his signal flag he walked in front of the Tank, directing it along the trench in a perfect hail of bullets and bombs. The machine-gun strong points were overcome, very heavy casualties were inflicted on the enemy, and a very critical situation was relieved.

By the spring of 1918 large numbers of American troops had arrived to support the war-weary Allied forces. Although Ludendorff publicly dismissed the presence of the inexperienced Americans, privately he knew they meant a military victory was no longer possible for Germany. Initially the Americans showed little interest in the concept of the tank. While they had a number of prototypes under development there was no great urgency to equip the American Army. However, the Americans were always swift to adopt new technology and Cambrai showed the way.

Although an American tank corps was formed, US industry was not in a position to supply it. Instead the Americans fielded British and French-built tanks. Just two days after the Amiens offensive opened the US 1st Army was created. American commander General John Pershing agreed with the Allied Supreme Commander General Foch that this would be used to attack the German St Mihiel salient south of Verdun on 12 September 1918. As well as gathering over half a million US troops Pershing's forces had the support of 419 tanks, about a third of which had American crews.

Lieutenant Colonel George Smith Patton Jr established the AEF's Light Tank School at the end of 1917. Following the Battle of Cambrai Patton was briefed by Colonel Fuller, Chief of Staff of the British Tank Corps. Then in the summer of 1918 Patton took command of the 1st Provisional Tank Brigade which was later re-designated the 304th Tank Brigade. This consisted of the 326th and 327th Tank Battalions equipped with French-supplied FT-17s.

Pershing's plan was to slice through the St Mihiel salient with attacks from the west and the south. American tanks were first deployed when Patton's tank brigade supported the US 1st and 42nd Divisions serving with 4th Corps to the south. His two battalions fielded 144 FT-17s, though the American attack was supported by a further 275 French tanks consisting of 216 FTs and fifty-nine Schneider and St-Chamond heavies. Short of manpower, the Germans had already begun to withdraw from the salient back to the Hindenburg Line before Pershing's operation commenced. By 13 September the US 1st and 26th Divisions had linked up and by the 16th the salient was under American control at a cost of 7,000 casualties.

Unfortunately Pershing's forces were then redeployed to conduct the Meuse-Argonne offensive in hilly, forested terrain that was not suitable for Patton's tanks. This attack was timed to coincide with British and French offensives and they withdrew much of their supporting equipment, leaving Pershing with fewer tanks and aircraft. To make matters worse, he had scarcely a week to prepare.

To reach the lateral railway from the Meuse-Argonne sector General Pershing's largely untried army, consisting of three corps, had to cover thirty miles. To do so they would first have to break through the German front. Then some eight miles behind it they faced the Kriemhilde sector of the Hindenburg Line. The French anticipated that the Americans would manage a third of the distance before winter.

While Pershing had every faith in his men, his confidence, like that of the French in 1914–15, was to founder on German machine guns.

Pershing's offensive opened on 26 September supported by 2,700 guns. Patton's tank brigade fought during the Meuse-Argonne operation with the US 1st Corps. While directing his tanks Patton was wounded attacking German machine guns near Cheppy. He continued to oversee his command from a shell crater for another hour before being evacuated. Patton would rise to the rank of four-star general and command of the US 3rd Army during the Second World War.

American tanks were also committed to battle elsewhere after the Meuse-Argonne offensive started. Forming part of the British 4th Tank Brigade serving under the Australian Corps, the US 301st Tank Battalion equipped with British Mark Vs suffered heavy casualties on 29 September during the Battle of the St Quentin Canal.

In the meantime the US 77th Division moved through the forests, assigned the task of linking up with the French on the west side. Although Montfaucon was taken by the US 79th Division on the second day, the central 5th Corps only came up level with the two flanks corps and made little further progress that day. Pershing had shot his bolt and in the days that followed the arrival of fresh German divisions enabled the enemy to counter-attack and force back the Americans in places. The French St-Chamond tank was involved in its last engagement in early October when sixteen were deployed to support the US 1st Division near Montfaucon. Pershing did not reach the southernmost part of the Hindenburg Line until 12 October.

In the closing months wrecked tanks still littered the battlefields. Fusilier Alexander Jamieson, 11th Battalion, Royal Scots Fusiliers following the Fifth Battle of Ypres said, 'As we advanced, we saw the terrible state of the Ypres salient. There were wrecked tanks from 1917 all over the place. I was used to the dead horses and mules, but not in the numbers that we saw up there. It was just shell holes everywhere ... We knew that things were going well.'

On 11 November 1918 the war finally came to an end when an exhausted Germany agreed to an armistice. Prime Minister Lloyd George recognized the role the tank had played in securing victory for the Allies, 'the tank attack [at Cambrai] showed clearly what an effective use could be made of these machines in overcoming the most formidable entanglements and entrenchments. This discovery was one of the principal factors in the German defeat of 1918.'

The tank had in some small measure contributed to Germany's downfall. It is evident that the tank concept had barely reached maturity by the end of the First World War. 'In essence the tank was only just moving into full series production when the war ended', notes historian Hew Strachan. Certainly in comparison to the numbers involved in the Second World War the quantity of tanks produced during the First World War were not great. Britain built around 5,000 heavies and the French 800, the Germans managed just twenty. France produced 3,000 light tanks that would greatly influence tank design during the 1920s and 1930s.

The British Tank Corps was designated the Royal Tank Corps in 1923. Then just before the outbreak of the Second World War it was renamed the Royal Tank Regiment (RTR), which formed part of the newly-formed Royal Armoured Corps. This was created by combining mechanized Regular and Territorial cavalry regiments with the RTR. After the First World War the Germans worked hard not to make the same mistakes again and in secret developed new panzers and the concept of Blitzkrieg. These were unleashed in September 1939 with devastating affect making them for a time the masters of Europe.

The AEF began to arrive in France in 1917, but initially it lacked tanks.

General John Pershing, commanding the AEF, was determined his troops would not be subordinate to the French. He also supported the creation of an American tank corps.

Lieutenant Colonel George Smith Patton Jr was tasked with setting up the US 304th Tank Brigade equipped with French-supplied FT-17s.

The US-manned FT-17s of the 326th and 327th Tank Battalions went into action against the German salient at St Mihiel south of Verdun on 18 September 1918.

American troops manning a French-supplied M1914 Hotchkiss machine gun.

US engineers at St Mihiel – the operation went very well. The Meuse-Argonne offensive did not.

American 'doughboys' and their tanks advancing over enemy trenches.

American-manned British Mark V heavy tanks of the US 301st Tank Battalion in action on the Western Front in 1918.

American tanks undergoing maintenance in the shelter of a forest.

Patton's tanks re-deploying for the Meuse-Argonne offensive. The lead tank is armed with a Hotchkiss machine gun while the one behind it has the Puteaux 37mm gun. Patton was wounded during this operation and showed great bravery.

Doughboys with a 37mm gun amongst shell-shattered trees. The Americans were subjected to fierce German counter-attacks at Argonne.

Doughboys storming a German bunker – the Meuse-Argonne offensive reached the Hindenburg Line on 12 October 1918.

US soldiers from the 7th Division celebrate news of the Armistice.

War's end – armoured cars of the 11th Hussars guarding a bridge over the Rhine in Cologne.